Organic Annie's
Green Gourmet Cookbook
Volume 1

Fresh Tastes
for Breakfast

Wheat and Dairy Free

Ann Miller-Cohen

green blessings,
Annie

Earth Angel Publishing
Manlius, NY 13104

Organic Annie's Green Gourmet Cookbook, Volume 1
Fresh Tastes for Breakfast, *Wheat and Dairy Free*
By Ann Miller-Cohen

Published by:
Earth Angel Publishing
4904 Briarwood Circle
Manlius, N.Y. 13104
www.organicannie.com

ISBN number 0-9765200-0-1

Disclaimer

This book is not intended as a substitute for the dietary or medical advice of physicians and other health-care providers. Rather it is intended to offer recipes and information to assist the reader who is working with a health-care professional in a joint quest for optimum health. Neither is the author/ publisher responsible for any products and/or services referred to in this book, or for any reactions that one might have upon preparing or consuming any of the foods referred to, or the recipes contained herein.

Front Cover design by Larry Sturgis
Photography by Ann Miller-Cohen
Verses by Ann Miller-Cohen

Printed in the United States of America.
First Printing

Dedication

To Earth and her children,
that seven generations hence
humankind will be healthier
in mind, body and spirit
than it is today.

Contents

Mother's Song

Feed me breakfast

feed me lunch,

feed me smooth,

feed me crunch,

feed me organic,

feed me wild,

feed me, Mother,

this is your child.

Kiss my boo-boo,

dry my eye,

make me laugh,

make me cry,

teach me

what's right from wrong.

Thank you, Mother,

this is your song!

Acknowledgments

To my sons, Shad Michael and Timothy Beech Miller, for being usually willing, sometimes reluctant and always honest taste-testers in our kitchen experiment stations in Baldwinsville, New York and beyond, and for the joy, awe and inspiration with which they have blessed my life. To Terry V. Miller, for being a patient and caring dad, and to his parents, Mary C. and O.J. Miller, for their wisdom and devotion to family.

To Nathan A. Cohen, my husband, dance partner and companion in the dance of life, for his love, support and encouragement. Without him this book might still be in the making.

To my mother, Frances E. Bukowski, for her passion for cooking and for her belief in me. To my step-father, Robert W. Bukowski, for his hard working example, and for his love for music and photography.

To the Oliver's and other friends, for perennially cajoling me to get my book done. To family, friends, clients and acquaintances from whom I have learned so much and who have believed in me and encouraged me in this endeavor over the years. To past friends and associates who literally died waiting for this book—their desire helped to keep the flames of my intention burning so that others might benefit from this work.

To Vickie and Paul Shufer for their patience and technical expertise; and to Joe Aquilino and the staff at Mercury Print Productions for handling this assignment with TLC. Together they got the genie out of the bottle!

To all organic and biodynamic growers and their families who labor with love, conviction and vision for a better world. And to all the people who support their vision. May the dream be made manifest!

To Mother Earth and Father Sky and to the Source of our greatest inspirations and highest aspirations.

I am gratefully indebted to All.

Ann Miller-Cohen

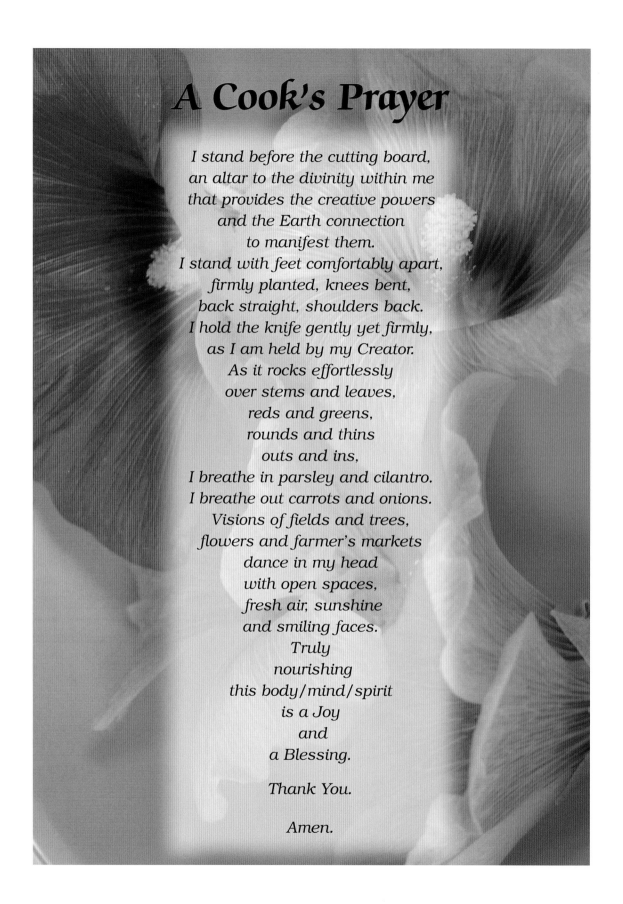

A Cook's Prayer

I stand before the cutting board,
an altar to the divinity within me
that provides the creative powers
and the Earth connection
to manifest them.
I stand with feet comfortably apart,
firmly planted, knees bent,
back straight, shoulders back.
I hold the knife gently yet firmly,
as I am held by my Creator.
As it rocks effortlessly
over stems and leaves,
reds and greens,
rounds and thins
outs and ins,
I breathe in parsley and cilantro.
I breathe out carrots and onions.
Visions of fields and trees,
flowers and farmer's markets
dance in my head
with open spaces,
fresh air, sunshine
and smiling faces.
Truly
nourishing
this body/mind/spirit
is a Joy
and
a Blessing.

Thank You.

Amen.

Introduction

It's a funny thing about life. If you refuse to accept
anything but the best, you very often get it.

--Somerset Maugham

I have written this book because of the profound impact that food choices have had on my life and the lives of those around me. Food has the power to heal or to maim, to clear the head or to cloud it, to lift the spirit or to burden it. As my wise teacher used to say, "Food is that which you eat or that which eats you!"

There is little that interacts with our physiology more intimately than the emotions we feel, the thoughts we think and the foods we eat. The love and caring that vibrate into these foods from the preparer are profound, albeit elusive aspects of this interaction. The gratitude of the eater, the receiver of the blessing, is equally powerful and important. Thus, for food to be truly healthful, the preparer must intend it to be so, and the eater must give thanks.

The kitchen, the place where food is prepared, is therefore a holy place, as well as a place of inspiration, fire and passion that befits its role in the creation of new flesh and blood, new thoughts and feelings. It is a place of healing and transformation, a place where we can make our dreams realities. It is a laboratory, a pharmacy, a testing and a proving ground. The aroma*therapy* that results provides us with a feeling of well-being and memories to last a lifetime. The practical side of healing begins here in a marinade of love, nature, knowledge, intuition and action.

So, if you are being forced to spend more time in the kitchen to deal with some special dietary needs look at it as a blessing and an opportunity. Yes, dietary "restrictions" can change your world, but do not assume the worst, for rather than contracting it, they can expand it by leading you to explore new foods, new ways, new relationships—new life!

When I was a little girl and would complain to my mother about something, she would remind me about "the man who cried that he had no shoes until he met a man who had no feet." While I could sympathize with the shoeless guy, Mom got her point across. The secret of coping successfully with any kind of restriction is to first, be grateful for what you have—focus on what you can eat, not on what you cannot. This immediately changes your attitude and opens the door to creativity and abundance.

Optimistically confronting my personal food challenges has improved my life physically, mentally and emotionally. Eliminating or minimizing wheat, dairy and sugar has also helped my sons and many of my clients to become healthier and happier. So we do not heal alone. In a very real sense, as we heal ourselves we heal the planet because this is a vibrational universe and the ripple effect is *humongous*!

Over the past 20 plus years, I have been developing recipes that will make it easier for you to make a transition by substituting some new foods for old standbys and by using some familiar foods in new, more healthful ways. I have not sacrificed flavor, for eating is one of the simple pleasures of life.

I have tried to present the most up to date information and best preparation methods that I know. Also, I have tried to share concepts so that you may exercise your own creativity and meet your own unique needs. In the beginning, try to stick to the recipes—at least until you get a taste and feel for what this way of eating is about. But enough said, an adventure awaits you.

The beginning of all things lies still in the beyond,
in the form of ideas that have yet to become real.

--the *I Ching*

What's a Green Gourmet?

Green, in our current vernacular, means clean, environmentally aware and responsible. *Green* is also the color for the heart chakra. It represents love and healing. I have heard it poetically and profoundly called "*the color of the Will living in Truth.*" It is also a color that the Creator has chosen for our Earth's mantle—for the chlorophyll rich plants that support terrestrial life. It is said that people who love *green* will work for free—the years I have taken to write this book bear witness to that, but truly it has been a labor of love! We will work without pay, but *for* something.

Webster's dictionary defines a *gourmet* as "an epicure: a judge of choice foods." It is flavor, as well as wholesomeness and sustainability that make foods "choice" for the *Green Gourmet*. To eat to be our best in body, mind and spirit is to revere and celebrate the Earth and the gifts she offers to balance, maintain and heal us. Thus the *Green Gourmet* is interested in personal and planetary health and chooses foods grown by Earth friendly production practices, like organics and biodynamics.

A *Green Gourmet* recognizes that you cannot improve upon nature, only perfect your knowledge and practice of her principles. Thus, I am suggesting that your food be as close to its natural state as practicable, with much of it eaten raw and the rest minimally processed and/or cooked for safety, palatability and digestibility.

Over-processing food takes its heart and soul away and leaves a vacuum that sucks nutrients from us in order for our bodies to process the lifelessness. No wonder we are not satisfied—we have not been nourished on any level. In contrast, whole foods, simply prepared, by ourselves or a loved one, can nourish and satisfy mightily!

Anyone with such a global vision as a *Green Gourmet* is also a busy person, so these recipes aim to be simple and quick. Yet, I would call them "slow food" because many of them require some presoaking of ingredients. *Slow food*--the movement--also embraces sustainability and stewardship of our natural resources, and honors the relationships and social institutions, the culture and history, behind preparing and sharing food.

So, a *Green Gourmet* is a health, socio-cultural and environmental activist just by the food and preparation choices s/he makes! What could be better than delicious, easy to prepare foods that enhance and maintain your health, support your values and protect the future generations of all species on this precious Earth? A *Green Gourmet* is improving the world and her/himself, one meal at a time!

Organic and Biodynamic

In this book, *organic* refers to foods that are grown, harvested, stored and marketed *without* industrial or municipal wastes, synthetic pesticides, herbicides, fungicides, growth hormones, preservatives or antibiotics and *with* organic and natural soil amendments and practices such as composting, liquid manures, companion planting, crop rotation, biodiversity and predatory insect controls.

The USDA's National Organic Program website says it this way:

Organic food is produced by farmers who emphasize the use of renewable resources and the conservation of soil and water to enhance environmental quality for future generations. Organic meat, poultry, eggs, and dairy products come from animals that are given no antibiotics or growth hormones. Organic food is produced without using most conventional pesticides; fertilizers made with synthetic ingredients or sewage sludge; bioengineering; or ionizing radiation. Before a product can be labeled "organic," a Government-approved certifier inspects the farm where the food is grown to make sure the farmer is following all the rules necessary to meet USDA organic standards. Companies that handle or process organic food before it gets to your local supermarket or restaurant must be certified, too.

From www.ams.usda.gov/nop

Biodynamic farming is based upon the Rudolf Steiner anthroposophical teachings on holistic and sustainable organic agriculture, first put forth in 1924. It is the oldest non-chemical agricultural movement, and enjoys a worldwide following including international standards and certification by the Demeter Association. Biodynamics is a sensitive approach that includes organic practices as well as energy balancing. For more information go to www.demeter-usa.org.

See "How to Read Produce Labels" on p. 55.

The Green Gourmet Kitchen

Grating apples with *Saladmaster*'s "Kitchen Machine"

Food Check List

Be sure to stock your kitchen with a variety of the following, organically or biodynamically grown foods:

- ✓ Fresh produce—local and seasonal is nice, but do not restrict yourself
- ✓ Dried unsulphured, unsweetened fruits
- ✓ Nuts and seeds—raw, unprocessed
- ✓ Sea vegetables from reputable suppliers
- ✓ Non-irradiated teas, herbs, spices and condiments
- ✓ Fresh eggs and animal products, if well tolerated
- ✓ Some frozen, unsalted, unsweetened foods for convenience
- ✓ Whole grains that are well tolerated
- ✓ Cold-pressed oils, e.g. olive and flaxseed
- ✓ Local raw honey and other natural sweeteners (**Appendix 1**)
- ✓ Sun dried sea salt

Equipment Check List

- ✓ A water treatment system, e.g. filter, R-O, and/or distiller
- ✓ Glass 1 gallon water jugs, or larger for water storage
- ✓ A blender with a glass container and at least 2 speeds
- ✓ A stainless, or other non-aluminum, food grater/cutter
- ✓ Strainers and colanders, non-aluminum
- ✓ A citrus juicer, glass or hard plastic, e.g. *Oxo*
- ✓ Glass bowls with lids and glass canning jars of various sizes for food storage
- ✓ Wooden and/or hard plastic stirring spoons, and spatulas
- ✓ A pair of chopsticks, for dislodging food around blender blade
- ✓ Sharp knives, e.g. *Cutco*
- ✓ Rubber scrapers
- ✓ Glass liquid measuring cups and plastic or stainless dry measuring cups and utensils
- ✓ Glass mixing bowls
- ✓ Stainless steel*, porcelain coated cast iron, or glass pots and baking dishes e.g. *Revere*, *Le Creuset* or *Pyrex*, respectively
- ✓ Cups, plates and serving dishes of glass or food grade ceramics

* Replace any that is scratched or pocked, for these can leach toxic heavy metals.

Setting the Scene

Setting the Scene

Breakfast is so named because we are *breaking the fast* since we last ate the day before. While it needs to be relatively easy and quick to prepare, nourishing and satisfying, it also needs to digest easily for we cannot afford to grind the wheels to a halt now, after all, we're just getting started!

Though breakfast may seem, at first, to be a difficult meal for someone on a wheat- and/or dairy-free diet, there are many options once we venture beyond the usual fare, besides it is too important a meal to miss. It helps to maintain optimal blood sugar, sustains both mental and physical energy levels, assists with weight control and acid/alkaline balance and more. Food manufacturers are also creatively responding to the demand with more and better products, so you will be happy that you made the effort.

This book, focuses mainly on recipes for *vital foods*. They are mostly raw, grainless, cleansing foods that are high in natural enzymes and *life force*. They are filling yet light on the digestive tract. **Volume 2** will focus on the more traditional, cooked breakfast foods--like cereals, pancakes, waffles and muffins—made without wheat or dairy products.

While anyone might benefit from the breakfasts in **Volume 1**, children, and persons with good health and strong digestion, or who are very active, or who work hard physically, might prefer or even require the heavier breakfasts in **Volume 2**.

Natural Rhythms

Our bodies have a natural rhythm of cleansing, digesting and assimilating. Breakfast falls into the period of cleansing. From 4 A.M. to 12 Noon, our bodies are in this mode. It is during this period that we do most of our internal housecleaning: sneeze, hack, blow, void copious amounts of urine, and move our bowels. Eating cooked foods that require the body to create digestive enzymes during this period will hinder the cleansing/ detoxifying process that would naturally be occurring.

What if you sleep days and work nights? Pay attention to your internal rhythm. Where is your cleansing cycle? When is your digestion strongest?

If one has a digestive weakness or a serious auto-immune or degenerative condition, it is helpful to generally eat a raw or liquid breakfast and to save the cooked food for noon or later, when the "digestive fires" are burning hotter. These people may benefit most from the recipes in this volume.

Body Rhythm

4 A.M. to 12 Noon—cleansing/detoxifying
12 Noon to 8 P.M.—digestion of nutrients
8 P.M. to 4 A.M.—assimilation of nutrients, rebuilding, renewal.

Thus, for many of us, the cooked portion of our daily diet is best taken between Noon and 8 P.M. Food taken after 8 P.M. should be light and occasional.

Food Combining and Selection

Paying attention to your food combinations can make a remarkable difference in how you feel, look and function. The main suggestions that I have for food combining are:

1) avoid eating concentrated proteins with concentrated starches*
   e.g. animal proteins with potatoes, grain, bread or pasta
2) avoid eating raw fruit with cooked foods of any kind
3) eat melons alone

And when you are planning your meals and doing your shopping, go for fresh, deep colored fruits and vegetables. They have the greatest food value. The recipes in this book were designed with these things in mind, for in order for our foods to be of greatest benefit, they must digest well, provide all the necessary nutrients and leave us well balanced chemically.

---

* Vegetarians might also experience improved digestion from eating their grains and legumes at separate meals; both combine well with greens and non-starchy vegetables. For most, complementary proteins like beans and grains need only to be eaten in the same day, not at the same meal. The greater nutritional needs of pregnant women and children are the exception.

The *sine qua non*—an alkaline balance

Our bodies are constantly performing a balancing act for us to keep our chemistry in the right pH (potential hydrogen) range for our enzymes and all of our metabolic processes to function efficiently.

Good food choices and properly combined foods assist in the maintenance of a slightly alkaline blood pH and metabolic balance. When we are metabolically balanced we feel well, with patience and sunny dispositions, more energy and stamina, better immunity and hormonal balance. We sleep better, look better, heal faster and easily maintain a healthy weight. The recipes in this book will help you to expand upon your alkaline-forming food choices.

An alkaline-forming diet is high in:
> high quality water*
> pesticide- and chemical-free foods
> raw and/or minimally cooked fruits and vegetables,
>   especially the deep green leafy veggies
> enzyme rich, presoaked or sprouted nuts and seeds

An alkaline-forming diet is low in:
> toxic foods and additives
> overly cooked, processed, and refined foods
> foods to which there is allergy or intolerance

An alkaline-forming diet is right for your metabolic type:**
> Carb Type: 25% protein/15% fat/60% carbohydrate
> Mixed Type: 30%/20% fat/50% carbohydrate
> Protein Type: 40% protein/30% fat/30% carbohydrate

Eating this way will give you a feeling of wellbeing. It will make you resistant to infections and help to insure that your blood remains slightly alkaline without having to draw on your bone and tissue reserves. Protecting these precious minerals is important at any age.

---

* F.Y.I. Water processing technologies are available to increase its alkalinity, but the author has not experienced these products enough to endorse any particular one.

**See more about this on the next page.

Maintaining a Healthy Weight

One widely pervasive problem today, "carbohydrate addiction," is rooted in an unhealthy aversion to fats, based upon erroneous and misleading nutritional information. This fad has resulted in the over-consumption of starchy foods like breads, pastas and cookies and an increase in food cravings, mood swings, depression, hypoglycemia, obesity and diabetes, as well as other degenerative diseases related to over-acidity and essential fatty acid deficiency. But I believe that it is not so much the calories, but the source of the calories—the particular foods--and how the body deals with them that determines weight gain or loss.

Your Metabolic Type

The ideal ratio of proteins, carbohydrates and fats varies from person to person depending upon the rate at which the body metabolizes them. Pay attention to how these foods make you feel and function, for example if you feel sleepy after a protein meal you might be a carb type, while if you feel lethargic after a starchy meal you might be a protein type. For a self-test see *The Metabolic Typing Diet*, by William Wolcott and Trish Fahey, (2000).

Food Allergy-Addictions

The three most "allergy-addictive" foods are wheat, dairy and sugar. Interestingly, most of our processed convenience foods contain one or more of these ingredients. Any amount of an allergy food can overcome the most "Herculean willpower" by triggering allergy-addiction, according to nutritional psychologist and author, Julia Ross, M.A. This is why diets that include even small amounts of these foods fail for so many of us.

In addition to the problems of carbohydrate and allergy-addictions, grains are generally quite acid-forming and refining and overly processing them makes them even more so. For more on the problem with grains, see *The Diet Cure*, by Julia Ross, M.A. (1999), *Going Against the Grain*, by Melissa Diane Smith (2002) and *Dr. Mercola's Total Health Cookbook and Program*, by Dr. Joseph Mercola, et.al (2004).

A Brief Summary of Blood Type Diet Recommendations

While foods like corn tend to encourage weight gain for all blood types, blood type diets go further to eliminate food proteins (lectins) that your body will attack as antigens depending on your type.

- O—meat eater (high stomach acid), does well with a "Caveman Diet;" does poorly with dairy, wheat and most grains. O's who choose to be vegetarians will need to limit starchy foods and work at getting enough protein and high quality fats to maintain good health.
- A—intolerant to red meats (low stomach acid) and dairy, can do well on a vegetarian diet. A's should avoid bananas and most other tropical fruits.
- B—an omnivore (moderate stomach acid), tolerant to cultured dairy, meats and some whole grains. Intolerant to chicken (turkey is okay) and most seeds, though flaxseed are beneficial. (Chia seeds are not mentioned in the Blood Type books.)
- AB—mixed diet in moderation (low stomach acid), shares many strengths and weaknesses with A and B types.

Because there is an immune response to foods that are not type-compatible, habitually eating these foods can lead to much more serious problems than weight gain. For more information also see, *Live Right 4 Your Type* and the *Eat Right 4 Your Type Encyclopedia* by Peter D'Adamo, N.D., or visit the website www.4yourtype.com.

"Volumetrics"

It is being shown that diets high in foods with low calorie density, i.e. foods that contain a lot of water and fiber*, help us to achieve and maintain healthy weight by filling us up rather than out. Barbara Rolls, author of *The Volumetrics Eating Plan*, professor and director of the Laboratory for the Study of Human Ingestive Behavior at Pennsylvania State University, has found that her subjects tend to eat the same volume of food daily, regardless of the calories. Thus, fresh vegetables and fruits, salads and soups are promoted for weight loss programs for their high volume but low calorie density.

* The *fruit and fiber* recipes in this book fit into this category. Even the nuts and seeds, which are high in calories due to their beneficial and heart-friendly fats, are handled in a way that increases their volume and water.

Recipe Overview

Fresh *Fruit and Fiber Breakfast* with Homemade *Almond Milk*

Recipe Overview

This book contains recipes for what I refer to as *fruit and fiber* breakfasts. Here you will find water based beverages and raw, enzyme rich nut and seed milks, fruit salads and smoothies, high fiber s/cereals, and lightly cooked breakfast puddings. There are few grain recipes in this volume.

There is a popular misconception that raw/*living* foods are difficult to digest, and/or   are a source of contamination. This is only true in some parts of the world where farmers still fertilize with "night soil," human wastes. Where foods are grown with acceptable organic and biodynamic fertilizers, raw foods are safe, in fact they are superior to cooked food in the energy that they have to impart to the eater.

This is because raw foods increase the *bio-electric potential* of the cells and thus restore a high level of function—absorption of nutrients and excretion of toxins. Per Dr. Gabriel Cousens, M.D. (*Conscious Eating*), "by restoring the electrical potential of cells, raw foods rejuvenate the life force and health of the organism."

So, if you are experiencing ill health, or low energy without a detectable cause, or if a traditional cooked breakfast leaves you feeling like Mark Twain's lead-bellied jumping frog—full of potential but unable to "hop to it"--these lighter breakfasts can be transformative. They are delicious, filling and have the right mix of nutrients to sustain you until lunchtime.

Other advantages of eating this way

> ➤ For a person on a wheat- and dairy-free diet, these foods will increase your breakfast options. Variety is always fun and we get a better array of nutrients, including as yet unidentified phytonutrients, when we eat a varied diet.

> ➤ Raw foods have greater food value because their nutrients have not been damaged by heat and processing.

> ➤ We are, generally, more acidic in the morning and need a little alkalizing start. These raw breakfasts tend to be alkaline-forming, while traditional breakfast fare tends to be acid-forming.

➤ These foods have a high water and fiber content thus they assist in healthy weight management even as they are cleansing and beneficial to the digestive tract.

➤ They enable those who enjoy fruit to "have their fruit and eat it too," while still maintaining blood sugar and energy balance.

Foods included in these recipes

Beverages: pure water, herbal teas, raw freshly made juices and green drinks for lubricating, cleansing and alkalizing.

Fruit: raw or lightly cooked fresh fruit and plumped (reconstituted) dried fruit for flavor, nutrients and fiber.

Nuts and seeds: including various products made from them (milk, cream and yogurt) for protein, live enzymes, beneficial fats, flavor and staying power.

Gel-forming seeds (soluble fiber foods): for providing smooth textures and bulk, and for cleansing and soothing the digestive tract, balancing blood sugar and lowering LDL cholesterol.

Various types of bran: providing both soluble and insoluble fibers for lowering LDL cholesterol and for the filling and cleansing effects of dietary bulk.

Ingredient Notes

My definition of dairy products is foods produced by dairy cattle, thus I do not consider eggs to be dairy.

Wheat bran is listed as an option in a few recipes because some persons sensitive to the starchy endosperm of wheat seem to tolerate the bran covering when used in this way.

Chapter 1

Water—the Elixir of Life!

Water—the Elixir of Life!

Pure water, the *universal solvent*, the original "*miracle grow*," is the best beverage and the easiest. Provide high quality water in your home and train yourself and your family to drink it regularly. It will assist with natural weight control and detoxification, keep the joints lubricated and the whole system humming. Our health is largely a matter of water and how it is distributed in our bodies. We need to be constantly replenishing our water to maintain adequate hydration*.

Water is also the quintessential ingredient for cleaning and preparing foods and other beverages. Cooking or otherwise "processing" food is all about water—retaining it, increasing it, or reducing it--in the finished product. For the best results start with the best water and the best ingredients!

Providing Safe Water

Not only do we need to ingest enough water but it needs to be clean and safe. Ironically, municipally "treated" tap water is often neither for it may contain chlorine, industrial grade fluoride and possibly heavy metals and other contaminants, including an alarming array of disease causing anaerobic microbes: bacterias, amoebas and protozoans.

All home purification/filtration systems are designed to at least remove chlorine, which can bond with organic substances creating carcinogenic compounds. Water purification systems demonstrate varying degrees of effectiveness with other contaminants, and most will not remove fluoride. See the manufacturer's specs for what a system claims to remove. Carbon block filters, like *Britta* and *PUR*, are the simplest and will at least eliminate chlorine.

---

* It is generally agreed that we need to drink at least half our body weight in ounces of water daily. For instance, someone who weighs 150 lbs., needs to drink 75 oz., or 9½ - 8 oz. glasses of water per day. Dr. Joseph Mercola, host of the nutritional website, www.mercola.com, recommends that we consume 1 quart daily for every 50 lbs. of body weight, or 3 quarts (12 8oz. glasses) for 150 lbs. Note: Sub-clinical dehydration has been blamed for many of the problems of mankind. See *Your Body's Many Cries for Water*, by Dr. Batmanghelidj, M.D.

A Little Controversy...

Dr. Joseph Mercola, D.O., recommends reverse-osmosis systems (RO), including a pre- and post-filtration system which is more complete—removing virtually all contaminants, including fluoride. Mercola, however, cautions on the use of distilled water which he says "has the wrong ionization, pH, polarization and oxidation potentials, all of which damage your health and drain minerals from your body."

Dr. Robert O. Young, biochemist and nutritionist, disagrees and writes that both RO and distilled water are alkaline. Distilled water, he writes in *The pH Miracle*, comes the closest to rain water, if our atmosphere was not so polluted.

For preparing foods, I prefer steam distilled water because it is thirsty for nutrients and will absorb more flavor. If one has unhealthy mineral deposits, such as bone spurs, drinking distilled can be therapeutic.

Drinking exclusively distilled water can be problematic, especially when one is under a lot of stress, mineral deficient or is on a poor diet that does not provide adequate minerals. Minimizing sweets and eating a lot of dark green leafy vegetables and several servings of sea vegetables weekly can help to bring the body back into balance without the need for mineral supplements which are often poorly absorbed.

What's Wrong with Fluoride in Municipal Water?

Fluoride has been promoted by the American Dental Association and the U.S. Public Health Department as a means of reducing cavities, since the 1940's when it was discovered that the people from a small area in Texas, which had naturally occurring fluoride in its drinking water, had better than average teeth. Unfortunately, what is being added to our public water supply is not the same; it is derived from industrial waste.

Fluoride concentrates when water is boiled, unlike chlorine which vaporizes. Thus its concentration in teas, soups and anything that is cooked for a long time in water, can exceed the 4 ppm (parts per million) that the EPA considers safe and acceptable. Fluoride makes bones and teeth hard and dense, but creates a brittle hardness, not the tensile strength that we need overtime. It also destroys enzymes in our bodies.

Is fluoridated public water playing a role in the present obesity epidemic in the U.S.? Dr. Mercola says that fluoride "can act as a metabolic poison and damage your thyroid" (*The No-Grain Diet*). Endocrinologist Stephen Langer (*Solved: the Riddle of Illness*) maintains that "since 1854, it has been known that fluoride is one of the most potent inhibitors of thyroid function, particularly where there is a low to deficient iodine concentration" in the soil in which food is grown e.g. the "Goiter Belt" of the U.S.

Persons who would like to include natural fluorine sources in their diets may consume green or black tea (*Camellia sinensis*), sunflower seeds and canned fish (with bones). (See the box at the bottom of this page.)

Bottled Water

No matter what system you choose, it is advisable to minimize the use of bottled water and to avoid drinking water out of the following plastic bottles for they leach toxic chemicals: #3--polyvinyl chloride (PVC), #6--polystyrene (PS) and #7--polycarbonate. Better plastics are #1, 2, 4, and 5. Long storage (over 6 months) or exposure to high temperatures in any plastic will increase leaching of toxic chemicals.

For a recently published exposé of fluoride, see *The Fluoride Deception*, by Christopher Bryson, (2004).

For more information visit the website of *The Fluoride Action Network* at www.fluoridealret.org.

F.Y.I. The homeopathic cell salt, *Calcarea Fluorica 6X*, may be taken as a supplement; it has a lactose base.

Beverages

While our cells benefit most from plain, pure water*, flavoring water adds variety and helps us to consume adequate amounts. If we choose wisely, beverages may also boost our intake of vital nutrients. Simple, subtle flavorings can be the most healthful, like a squeeze of fresh lemon or lime juice, or a few wedges of fruit.

Cold Drinks

"Cold" drinks are best taken at room temperature, preferably not iced. They are not shocking to the system this way, so will not slow down the digestive process. It is especially important to avoid really cold beverages at times of respiratory challenge, though cold drinks may be beneficial in an emergency to help bring down a fever.

Fruit Waters

My Latin American friends introduced me to these refreshing drinks. You can make them by blending about 1 cup of fresh fruit with 1 to 2 cups of pure water, strain to remove seeds, if desired, and drink. They contain less sugar than juice, yet offer variety and more nutrients than plain water.

Watermelon Drink

This is a sweet and refreshing summer beverage, cleansing and rich in carotenes, including lots of lycopene. Blend watermelon chunks until you have a thick puree. Be sure to include seeds and pieces of the white rind (peel off the green outer rind) for their protein content. Thin with an equal amount of pure water. Strain, if desired.

---

* Teach children the value of drinking pure water. It will keep their teeth and bodies healthy and insure a beneficial life habit. Carbonated beverages (except for naturally carbonated waters) are net losses nutritionally and should be avoided by all.

Green Drinks

Green vegetables are among the most alkalizing and cleansing of foods. Greens are also rich in vitamins and minerals; they are easy to digest and slenderizing. I believe that God clothed the Earth in green because these plants are meant to be our food and medicine.

The chlorophyll in green plants produces oxygen in the presence of sunlight. In our bodies it helps to build red blood cells because of its similarity to hemoglobin. Thus, chlorophyll is a blood builder. Consuming chlorophyll rich plants improves our blood's ability to carry oxygen, and to rid our cells of acid wastes* providing all around improvements in health and wellbeing.

- Green drinks help many with their weight loss programs because one reason for obesity is over-acidity, per Dr. Robert O. Young, biochemist and author of *The pH Miracle*.

An easy and delicious way of getting more green power into your diet is to make "Green Drink." Its pineapple juice base makes it delicious to most—even those who are "put off" at first by its beautiful jade color. Of course, it may be made with other juices or with plain water.

Green Drink

Yields 2 quarts or more*

2 c. water
1 qt. raw greens** (try half romaine lettuce and half spinach, chard, cilantro or parsley)
1 – 12 oz. can frozen pineapple juice, thawed
1 qt.+ pure water

Carefully select greens, wash under running water and coarsely chop; place in the blender with 2 cups of water. Affix cover and hold it down; turn to low then increase speed as the pieces become finer. Blend until the liquid is dark green.

Strain through cheesecloth or mesh strainer into a non-metallic container. Pour strained green juice into a 2 quart jug. Add thawed juice and stir, then add enough water to fill to the top. Affix lid and shake to mix juice. Shake again before serving. Drink within 24 hours for the greatest benefit.

Variations: Replace pineapple with orange or other juice. For a totally raw, high enzyme beverage, replace frozen concentrate with 5 to 6 cups of cubed raw pineapple***. Add it to the blender along with greens. After straining, add enough water to make at least 2 quarts. Powdered super foods (below) may also be added to boost nutrients.

---

* You may prefer to add an extra quart of water to make 3 quarts from a 12 ounce can of concentrate, to dilute the fruit sugar. It will still taste good.

**Avoid raw cabbage family greens like turnip tops, mustard greens and cabbage; these contain a natural chemical (goitrogen) which blocks iodine absorption in the thyroid, causing hypothyroidism—low output.

***Raw pineapple contains bromelain, an enzyme that helps to break down proteins and, when taken on an empty stomach, soothes inflammation.

Green Drink for One

1 c. water
1 c. fresh pineapple, cubed
1 large handful fresh greens as above

Combine all in the blender at once. Process for a couple of minutes. Strain and drink.

Variation: If fresh pineapple is not available, process the water and greens and strain, then stir in 2 to 3 Tbsp. pineapple or other concentrate. Or replace fresh pineapple with a cup of orange, carrot or other juice, preferably freshly squeezed.

Green Drinks from Super Foods

Super foods, or power foods, contain higher concentrations of beneficial alkalizing and detoxifying nutrients and phytonutrients than other foods commonly eaten. For this reason I suggest that adults, especially, find ways to incorporate them into their demanding lives.

Stir a total of 1 teaspoon to 1 tablespoon of the powdered form of any one or a combination of the following into a pint jar or tumbler of water, juice, or *Rejuvelac* (directions on next page):

> spirulina
> chlorella
> wheat grass
> barley grass
> kamut grass
> alfalfa leaf

Affix lid and shake to mix. You might want to start out with a little and gradually increase as you acquire a taste for it. I like to add a *drop* of organic peppermint oil.

Note: All of these super foods—even the grasses--are gluten-free.

Rejuvelac—a fermented beverage

One of the foundations of Dr. Ann Wigmore's *living foods* diet was rejuvelac, which she considered an elixir for the digestive tract. It is a fermented beverage made by soaking sprouted grains in pure water. It develops a nice fizz. Good rejuvelac, in fact, tastes like champagne! From my experience quality can vary a lot, but the best results can be attained by keeping the culturing room temperature around 70 to 72° F. Fermentation proceeds too slowly at lower temperatures and too rapidly at higher temperatures.

Rejuvelac can be drank as is, or used as the base for green drinks or Energy Soup, dressings, sauces, dips and the starter for the fermentation of other foods like nuts and seeds. Dr. Ann used to say that rejuvelac could purify water. It is also filled with vitamins B, C and E and enzymes. She recommended to begin a fresh batch daily.

Directions for Making Rejuvelac

Yields about 3 cups

1 c. spelt (the original recipe called for spring wheat)*
3½ c. distilled water
½ tsp. citric acid (optional—to kill mold)

Pour grain into a mesh strainer and rinse under running water, moving your hand through the grain in a circular motion. In a 1 quart jar combine: grain, water (to the shoulder of the jar) and citric acid. Let stand for 8-10 hours. Drain and rinse grain.

Now spread them out in a plastic or nylon mesh colander (over a bowl to catch drips) and cover loosely with a clean towel. Sprout for 2 days, rinsing three times daily.

Put the sprouts back into a clean quart jar and fill with fresh, purified water (no citric acid this time). Cover and let it work for another day. If the smell and taste are agreeable, refrigerate and use 1 cup or more daily.

---

* If there is gluten-intolerance try a gluten-free grain, however, many grains will not sprout because their protective outer coatings have been removed in processing. In that case eliminate the sprouting step.

Cold Herbal Teas

Herbal teas can provide much needed water replacement while providing nutrients that cleanse, strengthen and balance body systems. The following contain no caffeine unless otherwise noted. Teas can be made by *decoction* (cooking) or by *infusion* (steeping). Always use unsprayed, preferably organically, or bio-dynamically, grown fruits, herbs and flowers. When using fresh herbs, usc 2 to 3 timcs as much as dried.

Sun tea is a "cold" infusion that depends upon sunlight to draw the essential oils and nutrients into the water. (Only fresh or freeze-dried ingredients contain the beneficial volatile essential oils.)

Basic Sun Tea
Yields 1 quart

1 qt. distilled water, room temperature
1 c. fresh herbs and flowers, organically grown or at least unsprayed

Combine all ingredients in a clear glass quart jar, affix lid and set in a sunny place for 2 to 4 hours. Strain and drink, or store in the refrigerator.

A Touch of Grace, A Touch of Color

Edible flowers can be added to Sun Teas or used to make delicate, colorful garnishes for all kinds of foods, from beverages to desserts.

Choose from organically grown: roses, marigolds, dandelions, peppery nasturtium and mustard flowers (including dame's rocket), peonies, violets, pansies, daylilies, mallows, mints, leeks and onions, sorrel.

Shake, or spritz whole blossoms with a gentle cold water spray to debug and wash. Shake or spin out moisture.

Flower and Fruit Sun Tea

Yields about 3½ quarts

Place the following in a clear glass gallon jug, then fill with cool water:

1 handful chrysanthemum flowers (dried)
4 dried pineapple slices, unsulphured, unsweetened
½ c. hibiscus flowers (dried)
¾ c. elderberries (dried)

Affix a lid and set out in a sunny place for 2 to 4 hours. Strain and serve over ice or chilled. Sweeten with a little fruit juice concentrate if desired.

Peony Mint Tea

Yields 1 quart

Place the following in a clear glass quart jar, then fill with cool water:

1 freshly picked peony flower head
a small handful of fresh mint leaves

Affix a lid and set out in a sunny place for 2 to 4 hours. Strain and serve or chill, if desired.

The following is an energizing and refreshing summer drink with an unexpected zing.

Jungle Tea

Yields about 3½ quarts

Place the following in a clear glass gallon jug, then fill with cool water:

3 sprigs parsley
a few leaves of spinach, or wild lamb's-quarters
4 leaves of fresh sage
a small handful each fresh rosemary and oregano herbs
8 marigold flower heads
1 medium hot red pepper, quartered lengthwise (remove seeds)
⅓ c. hibiscus flowers (dried)
4 dried pineapple slices, unsulphured, unsweetened
a few small dried mango slices, unsulphured, unsweetened

Affix a lid and set out in a sunny place for 2 to 4 hours. Strain and serve.

Hot Drinks

Hot drinks satisfy, comfort and relax, and may help us to stay healthy or to heal. Be sure not to drink them too hot for this will harm the little surface cells of your mucous membranes that work so hard to keep you well nourished and protected from foreign invaders and irritants. Simple hot water is drank around the world to gently awaken the digestive tract and for regularity.

Tree ripened lemons and limes are alkaline-forming and healing to the kidneys, liver and gall bladder. Lemons should be bright yellow, not greenish, and limes should be dark green. Save and use the peels of organically grown fruit for their flavor and health enhancing bioflavonoids and essential oils. (See p. 101.)

Hot Lemon- or Limeade
Serves 1

1 c. hot water
1 tsp. honey
1 to 2 Tbsp. fresh lemon or lime juice

In a teacup, dissolve the honey in hot water, then add the juice.

Beverages from Nuts and Seeds

Milks and smoothies made from nuts and seeds are also featured in this book, including *Hot Carob-coa, Melon Seed Drink, Pumpkin Seed Milk,* and *Squash Nog.* See **Nut and Seed Milks** in **Chapter 4**.

Tip: While I recommend freshly squeezed, organically grown citrus in season, if it is unavailable, or if you just need a quick serve, I suggest keeping some Minute Maid™ lemon juice (from pure concentrate) in the fridge. It is packaged in plastic squeeze bottles and may be found in the freezer case of your local supermarket (sold in a box). Though it is not made from organically grown lemons, it contains no sugar or preservatives.

*Blackstrap molasses is an end product of sugar refining. It is mildly sweet and high in bio-available iron and calcium. It looks like black coffee. It may be contaminated by pesticide residues from conventionally grown sugar cane, so buy organic (see chart of nutrients in **Appendix 1**). This may be made with plain hot water or added to herbal tea--it's particularly good in "Ginger Tea."*

Kids' Coffee

Makes 1 cup

1 tsp. blackstrap molasses, unsulphured
1 c. very hot water

Place molasses in a teacup and stir in hot water.

If you are already taking some powdered herbs you might enjoy stirring them into blackstrap molasses before pouring in the hot water. The herbs stir in better this way and It makes bitter herbs more palatable. Always begin by using them singly to check your reaction.

My Meno-lasses Drink

Makes 1 cup

Place 1 tsp. blackstrap molasses in a cup and stir in any one, or up to 1 tsp. of a combination, of any of the following:
¼ tsp. chaste tree berry powder
¼ tsp. ground ginger
¼ tsp. marshmallow root powder
¼ tsp. dandelion root powder
¼ tsp. Siberian ginseng powder
¼ tsp. fenugreek powder

Pour hot water over and stir. Relax and enjoy.

For a Pick up: Stir in 1 to 2 tsp. of nutritional yeast flakes for protein and B-complex vitamins. Look for the *Saccharomyces cerevisiae* strain which does not promote *Candida*, but is immune supportive.

Hot Steeped Teas

Dense materials like barks and roots lend themselves to *decocting* to release their nutrients, while more delicate materials like leaves, flowers and fruits are best steeped (*infused*). 160° F. is the optimal steeping temperature for herbs and regular tea, *Camellia sinensis*.

Some popular caffeine-free herbs for steeped teas are: chamomile, mints, hibiscus, fenugreek (a seed), alfalfa, clover and ginger (grated root). Ground roasted roots and grains may also be steeped, e.g. chicory, dandelion and barley.

Basic Recipe for Steeped Tea

Makes 1 cup

1 tsp. dried herb, or 1 Tbsp. fresh herb
1 c. hot water

Pour hot water over herb and steep (allow to stand) for 5 to 10 minutes. Strain. Sweeten to taste.

Mints are widely distributed throughout the world and well known herbal tea plants. They offer minerals and aromatic essential oils, especially when fresh. Peppermint and lemon balm are popular stomach soothers. Catnip is relaxing and good for colicky infants and overactive kidlets. Avoid honey as a sweetener for children under 2 years of age. I suggest half fruit juice, half tea to sweeten. **Caution:** *Avoid peppermint tea after meals if you are experiencing heartburn or acid reflux.*

Mint Tea

Makes 1 cup

1 tsp. dried or 1 Tbsp. fresh leaves
1 c. hot water

Pour boiling water over leaves and steep for 5 minutes. Strain and drink hot or serve chilled.

Hibiscus grows wild in tropical climates. It imparts a sensual rosy color and tart, fruity flavor to many tea blends. You may also enjoy it by itself as a hot drink, or chill and combine half and half with fruit juice for a lovely and refreshing cold drink. It is quite alkalizing, but go easy, it is also diuretic.

Hibiscus Tea

Makes 1 cup

2 or 3 hibiscus flowers
1 c. hot water

Pour water over leaves and steep for 5 minutes. Strain, sweeten and drink or chill.

Ginger increases circulation, helps to break-up sinus and chest congestion and may soothe an upset stomach, motion sickness and intestinal cramps. Like some of the other herbs that begin with "G" (garlic, ginkgo, ginseng), ginger is a blood thinner.

Ginger Tea

Makes 1 cup

1 c. very hot water
1 tsp. to 1 Tbsp. fresh ginger root, peeled and finely grated

Combine in a tea cup and steep for 3 to 5 minutes. Sweeten if desired.

Variation: ¼ tsp. ground cardamom may be added to each cup for additional digestive aid.

I recommend a glass or porcelain coated pot for all tea preparations. Avoid the use of aluminum or copper pots.

The following tea may also be helpful for colds and congestion. It soothes inflamed mucus membranes with its healing mucilage. Swallow seeds whole to avoid irritation.

Flaxseed Tea
Serves 1

1 c. boiling water
2 to 3 tsp. whole flaxseed

Pour boiling water over the seeds and steep for 10 to 15 minutes.

Chicory flower

Chicory, a member of the composite family, is sweeter than you might think. It contains inulin, an indigestible carbohydrate that is beneficial to diabetics. The roasted root makes a "rich and robust," dark tea.

Chicory "Coffee"
Makes 1 cup

½ to 1 tsp. roasted chicory root, granules
1 c. very hot water

In a small pot, stir chicory into water. Let steep for 5 minutes or more. Strain and drink.

Overnight Teas

These *long infusions** are made by steeping overnight. This extracts more minerals from the plant material. Boil a quart of water and pour it over 1 ounce of the herb (about 1 cup) which has been placed in a 1 quart glass canning jar. Affix the lid and let steep for 4 to eight hours, or overnight. In the morning, strain and refrigerate what you will not be drinking right away. You may drink this tea at room temperature or warm it before serving (boiling not recommended). Look for these herbs in stores where natural foods are sold.

Alfalfa Leaf Tea *(Medicago sativa)*
With roots that can reach over 30 feet in depth, alfalfa is one of the most highly mineralized land plants.

Oat Straw Tea *(Avena sativa)*
Oat straw is a rich source of silica. It is strengthening to hair, skin and nails and calming to the nervous system. This tea tastes sweet and smooth. The best quality is from oats in the green milky stage. Use the top 6 inches. Purchase "green flowering" oat straw.

Stinging Nettle Tea *(Urtica dioica)*
Nettle is said to be the most highly mineralized land plant. It makes a dark rich tea that is strengthening and healing to the kidneys. It is helpful in pregnancy to raise the hematocrit and later in life to keep the hair dark and the skin smooth.

Red Raspberry Leaf Tea *(Rubus idaeus)*
Known mainly as a woman's herb, raspberry is high in minerals and good for the whole family. It also helps keep the immune system strong. Leaves for tea are harvested before the flowers bloom.

---

* For more information on long infusions and herbal preparations, see books by herbalist Susun Weed.

F.Y.I. These herbs can be ordered from Frontier Natural Products Co-op if not locally available. See **Appendix 2**.

Decocted (Cooked) Teas

Decocting is the preferred method for making teas of dense, hard materials like roots, twigs and barks. If you are starting with dried material I recommend to presoak it in water for several hours to soften it, then its nutrients will release more easily into the water and cooking time will be shortened.

This is my all time favorite tea. Serve it hot or cold. Ginger combines well with other herbs in beverages and in cooking. It is warming and aids digestion. See, also, the recipe for infused ginger tea above.

Ginger Tea

Makes 2 cups

Peel a 1" piece of fresh ginger root. Slice very thinly and add to 2 cups of cold water. Heat to simmering and maintain this heat for 15 to 20 minutes. Save the root pieces and simmer in 1 cup of water next time. Drink as is, or sweeten with a little honey. Children might find it more palatable combined half and half with fruit juice.

Kukicha twigs come from Camellia sinensis, the same plant that gives us green and black tea, however, it is considered suitable for children for it contains calcium and only a trace of caffeine. It could be drunk on alternating days with kombu tea as a remedy for Candida yeast overgrowth.

Kukicha Twig Tea

Yields 1 cup

1 tsp. kukicha twigs
1¼ c. cold water

Bring water to a boil and turn down to simmer for 10 to 15 minutes. Strain and drink. Sometimes I like it simmered with a few pieces of sliced ginger root and sweetened with blackstrap molasses.

The mineral rich cooking water or stock from any of the sea vegetables may be drank as a tea. Kombu* is a brown kelp. It is a source of most minerals including iodine and is good as a tea or soup base. It will help to alkalize the body and support the immune system. Pre-soak in a couple of cups of water for about 15 minutes. Drain and rinse under running water, then proceed with the recipe.

Kombu Tea

Yields about a quart

one 3" piece of kombu (kelp)
1 quart of water

Combine presoaked kombu and fresh water in a pot, cover and simmer for half an hour or more. Strain and drink. The kombu may be eaten or chopped and added to soups or salads.

This is cleansing, immune boosting and slightly diuretic. It is often recommended to help correct a Candida yeast imbalance.

Pau D'Arco (Taheebo) Tea

Makes 2 cups

2 c. water
2 tsp. pau d'arco bark, shredded

Combine and simmer in a covered pot, for 15 to 20 minutes. Strain and drink. Save the strained bark to be simmered again with 1 cup of water, next time.

---

* Sea vegetables are of great benefit for the dairy intolerant for they provide a wide array of both macro- and micro-minerals in a bio-available form.

Dandelion "hognose" characteristic of fresh blooms

Dandelion was brought to the new world by our ancestors who revered its healing properties. The following is helpful for constipation and improving digestion. Dandelion root is a cholagogue i.e. it enhances both bile formation and its release from the gall bladder into the small intestine, where it digests dietary fats and assists in stool formation.

Dandy Root Tea

Yields 2 cups

2½ c. water
2 Tbsp. dried, cut dandelion root, or ¼ c. fresh chopped root*

If time permits, combine water and dried roots and let stand overnight to soften the roots and reduce cooking time. Bring to a boil and turn down to simmer for 15 to 20 minutes. Remove from heat and let stand until the root pieces have fallen to the bottom. Strain and serve as is, or with a little blackstrap molasses. Save the roots and simmer with only 1 cup of water next time.

* Harvest your own roots from a natural, non-toxic lawn from late fall (after a hard frost), through early spring. They contain lots of stored sugars during this period and have the best flavor. Scrub, chop and dry, or freeze. Or purchase dried, *cut and sifted* roots.

Broths

Broths are the waters flavored by slowly cooking vegetables and meats. They are nutritious and versatile and a must for all cooks, serious or otherwise. Broths make it possible to "get the good" out of otherwise unusable ingredients. They also form the basis for delicious and deeply nourishing soups and sauces. And they are so simple and carefree that no one need to be without!

Broth may be made from anything edible and from much that is too woody, bony, gristly or cosmetically incorrect to be palatable or attractive served in a visible form. Some broths are therapeutic, others are convenient, but all broths offer more than plain water in a recipe. Start with at least 2 parts water to one part vegetable ingredients. Cover and simmer until the veggies are limp. Strain and discard the solids and drink, or store the broth for later use.

The following is mineral rich and good for aches and pains. For many, it is a much better way to begin the day than with tea or coffee. It is also satisfying while on a fast from solid foods.

Basic Alkalizing Broth

Yields a little less than 1 quart

1 qt. water
1 stalk celery
1 onion
1 c. potato peels*, cut ¼" thick
1 sliced carrot and/or beet

Coarsely cut celery and onion. Combine all ingredients in a 1½ qt. saucepan, preferably made of enameled cast iron. Bring to a boil, cover and simmer for 20 minutes to 1 hr. Add more water to keep veggies covered if necessary. Strain out veggies and discard—don't cry; the goodness is in the broth! Season with a little salt, or miso, if desired.

---

* The peel is the most nutritious part of the spud, containing potassium, iron, vitamin C and protein. It is alkaline-forming while the white, starchy part is acid-forming. If sensitive to the nightshade family, omit and add more of the other ingredients.

Miso

Miso, a culinary gift from the East, is a uniquely flavorful, salty, fermented soy product that contains beneficial, gut friendly lactobacillus, B-vitamins and is rich in complete protein and potassium. It provides a hearty flavor but may still be light and warming.

Most miso is made from the fermentation of soy beans with a grain and salt. The type of grain used gives the miso its distinctive flavor and name, thus we have *genmai* (rice), *mugi* (barley) and *hacho* (soy, only) miso, to name some commonly available. Store miso in the refrigerator after opening. Miso is *not* recommended for sodium restricted diets.

In his book *Fighting Radiation and Chemical Pollutants with Food, Herbs and Supplements*, Steven R. Schechter, N.D. recounts the combination of rice, miso and sea vegetables which was eaten by the survivors of Nagasaki and Hiroshima. But you do not have to wait for a nuclear explosion to enjoy miso soup. It is good for just about any condition, except where there is sodium sensitivity or imbalance.

Simple Miso Cup
Serves 1

1 c. very hot water, broth, or *Kombu Tea*
1 tsp. miso

Stir the miso into a tablespoon or two of water to dissolve it, then stir it into the hot liquid.

Always add miso to foods after cooking. Never heat over 180° F. for this will destroy the beneficial bacteria.

Chapter 2

Fabulous Fruit

Freshly harvested Finger Lakes' apples

Fabulous Fruit

The Creator has blessed humanity with an awesome variety of fruit that enchant the mind, inebriate the senses and titillate the taste buds. In this way the Master insures that we desire what is good for us.

We merely need to consume what is offered in a way that conserves the precious nutrients provided. Most fruit is best when tree or vine ripened, and consumed raw or lightly cooked. Some may be preserved by dehydrating—removing the water--and consumed reconstituted—by adding the water back. Dehydrated fruit contains concentrated sugars so should be eaten sparingly. Freezing conserves more nutrients than canning but still entails some losses over fresh. Fermenting is another method of *putting fruit by*, but is not the subject of this volume.

It is the purpose of this book to introduce you to some perhaps new and/or more beneficial ways of using fruit—ways that will expand your use and appreciation of them.

My response to those nutritional writers who are recommending that we generally avoid fruit because it causes flora imbalances, predisposing us to *Candida* and parasitic infections, is that fruit is too essential* to write off in this way and, besides, these digestive and immune problems are *created* by other foods, like sugar, overly processed junk foods, bad fats and too many grain products in the diet. Moderate fruit consumption is part of a balanced diet.

One might have to go easy on fruit for a period of healing, but one should not have to forgo fruit forever. Additionally, if fruit is combined with the gel-forming seeds and/or other seeds and nuts it might be better tolerated and its sugar will be more slowly absorbed into the bloodstream.

---

* For the nutrients in fruits and other foods, I recommend *Nutrition Almanac*, Fifth Edition, by Lavon J. Dunne (2002), U.C. Berkeley's *Wellness Foods A to Z* (2002), by Health Letter Associate, and *The Color Code: A Revolutionary Eating Plan for Optimum Health*, by James A. Joseph, Ph.D., Daniel A. Nadeau, M.D. and Anne Underwood (2002).

It has been said that we have a taste for sweet because our ancestors' *sweet teeth* led them to the fruit and vegetables with the highest food values. Sugars are at their peak at ripe maturity when a plant's nutrient profile is at its highest. Thus, fruit provides us with lots more than pleasant flavors, textures and eye appeal. They are packed with nutrients (some still unidentified), fiber and enzymes which nourish, detoxify and protect our cells.

Fresh fruit is generally alkaline-forming, some exceptions being cranberries and plums. A raw fruit meal can provide a third or more of your day's alkaline requirement and provide enzyme activity to aid digestion, thus freeing energy for use elsewhere, like in supporting the immune system and the process of detoxification. When it is raw, its fiber will more effectively cleanse the digestive tract, also. The cleansing/detoxification process is in full swing between 4 A.M. and 12 Noon so breakfast is a natural time to consume fruit.

Yet, many feel that fruit is not enough to hold them until noon. I agree. If eaten alone and in quantity, fruit will provide too much sugar, feed yeasts and other dysbacteria* and make us crave more food as we ride a blood sugar roller coaster.

Fruit and Fiber Breakfasts

There is a way to make a "square meal" of fruit. I call it a *fruit and fiber breakfast.* When combined with the compatible proteins, high quality fats and fiber from nuts and seeds, fruits can healthfully and deliciously fill a vacuum in the breakfast choices of a person on a dairy- and wheat-free diet. These beneficial fibers, proteins and fats will buffer the fruit sugars and provide the steady release of energy over time. They will also enhance the cleansing qualities of fruits. So you can still *have your fruit and eat it too!*

---

* Persons with severe blood sugar or bacterial flora imbalances e.g. diabetes, hypoglycemia, *Candida albicans*, may need to go easy and/or avoid fruit—especially sweet ripe fruit, like bananas, and dried fruit--until their health has improved. See *Fruit and Vegetable Smoothies* in **Chapter 5**; "Veggie Variation," under *Lightly Cooked Breakfast Puddings*, in **Chapter 6**; and *Green Drinks* in the *Beverages* section of **Chapter 1**.

Ingredients in a *Fruit and Fiber Breakfast*:

✓ **Liquid** for cleansing and good digestion--at least 1 to 2 cups consumed as pure water or herbal tea or mixed with other foods to make cereals and milks

✓ **Fruit** for flavor, texture, fiber, and nutrients--preferably organically grown, or at least unsprayed.

✓ **High fiber foods** for feeling full, stabilizing blood sugar and cleansing—include various types of *gel-forming* seeds and/or bran mixed with water to maximize their benefits.

✓ **Nuts* or seeds** for flavor, proteins, fiber, good fats and live enzymes—presoaked before eating or processing, to make them crisper, lighter and more digestible.

For example, start the morning with at least 1 cup of pure water, room temperature or warm. Do some stretching or a more vigorous workout, if preferred. Then make the following:

Apple Ambrosia

Serves one

2 Tbsp. ground flaxseeds
½ c. water
½ to 1 crisp apple
4 plumped figs
a handful of presoaked seeds or nuts
dash of lemon juice
1 tsp. grated organic orange peel (optional)

Stir water slowly into flaxseeds. Let stand for at least 5 minutes. Grate the apple, sprinkle with lemon juice and stir to mix. Slice and add figs, and nuts or seeds. Toss all ingredients together. Sprinkle with orange rind.

---

* Persons who must avoid nuts will find that the seeds contain similar nutrients and benefits.

Suggestion: See the Blood Type books by Dr. Peter J. D'Adamo, and familiarize yourself with the foods that are most beneficial for your blood type and those which should be avoided.

Some Thoughts About Fruit Juices

I feel that it is generally better to eat the whole fruit with all of its fiber and nutrient dense seeds rather than to juice it. When one is consuming fruit or sweet veggie juices, it is important to dilute the juice at least 50/50 with pure water or *Chia Gel* (recipe in **Chapter 6**), for the sugars are detrimental without the natural buffering effect of the fiber found in the whole food.

Commercially available, processed, i.e. heated juices are not as beneficial as freshly made for much is lost by heating, including enzymes, vitamin C and folic acid.

Avoid prolonged contact with metals to prevent leaching by fruit acids. Store juices in glass jars, with enameled lids—*Ball*™ canning jars are excellent for this purpose—and serve in glass or food grade ceramics.

It is a good idea to bring children up drinking mainly pure water rather than fruit juices. It will give them a habit that will facilitate healthy weight maintenance and provide many other health benefits throughout their lifetimes.

Grapefruit juice is easy to make and does not have to be diluted. Follow with a drink of plain water to rinse the fruit acids from your teeth. I like to eat the bioflavonoid rich pulp and seeds, too! (If taking medication, check with your physician for interactions.)

Don't Panic, Go Organic

In January 2003, The U.S. Center for Disease Control reported that American children had up to twice the levels of many pesticides as adults. A study at the University of Washington that March revealed that children on organic diets had one sixth the level of metabolized organophosphate pesticides as those on conventional diets.

We need to provide our children with organically grown produce whenever possible because the toxic sprays used to deter insects and inhibit fungi on conventionally grown fruits and veggies are even more harmful to children than to adults. This is due to their proportionally smaller size and higher dietary intake of fruit, their less developed systems of detoxification, and the vulnerability of their still developing brains and bodies. Long-term exposure to pesticides can interfere with a child's neurological and immune system development and is likely contributing to increases in childhood cancers and degenerative diseases (from *The Way We Grow*, by Anne Witte Garland).

Read labels and buy organic when it is available*. "The USDA's organic food label remains the all-around top choice in food certification, providing clear standards and third-party verification and supported by research showing that organic agriculture is better than conventional both for the environment and your health."**

Top 10 Veggies and Fruit to buy Organic

To reduce your family's pesticide ingestion, buy organic varieties of the following most contaminated produce.

Veggies: spinach, bell peppers, celery, potatoes and hot peppers
Fruit: peaches, apples, strawberries, nectarines and pears

Less contaminated conventionally grown foods are blueberries, plums, avocados, radishes and broccoli.

---

* Other terms, like "local", "sustainable" and "beyond organic" are used to describe practices not covered in the USDA's organic regulations. Go to the Consumers Union web site www.Eco-labels.org for definitions and assessments of new terms.

**From "Healthy Eating," by P.W. McRandle, in the November/December 2003 issue of *THEGreenGuide #99*, available on the web at www.thegreenguide.com.

First choice is always organically grown and fresh fruits. Though I believe in eating locally grown produce, in its season and even growing some of it yourself when possible, I do not recommend restricting your diet to only locally grown foods. Variety provides more than spice and one can benefit from the nutrients assimilated by plants from different soil types. Always wash produce, whether it is organically grown or not, to remove bacteria, mold and fungi spores and parasitic organisms.

Removing Pesticide Residues

If it is not possible to get organically grown produce, peeling fruit and veggies will remove surface pesticides and waxes which are sometimes impregnated with fungicides. Oil based pesticides can often be washed off the surface of produce with a veggie scrub brush, when appropriate, and any of the following:

✓ **Mild castille soap**, like *Dr. Bronner's*™
✓ **A few drops of dishwashing liquid**
✓ **Apple cider vinegar:** Dilute with water
✓ **Fruit and veggie scrubs**, per directions

Of course, peeling means a loss of nutrients and fiber found in the skins and systemic pesticides cannot be removed by peeling or scrubbing.

How to Read Produce Labels

Fruit and vegetable labels contain different PLU codes depending on whether the fruit or vegetable was conventionally grown, organically grown or genetically engineered. The PLU code for conventionally grown produce consists of four numbers, organically grown have five numbers prefaced by "9", and genetically modified (bioengineered) have five numbers prefaced by "8".

For example:
- Conventionally grown Golden Delicious Apples PLU: 4020

- Organically grown Golden Delicious Apples PLU: 94020

- Genetically modified Golden Delicious Apples PLU: 84020

Fruit is Tops in Antioxidants

At the request of the USDA, scientists at the Agricultural Research Service's Human Nutrition Research Center on Aging at Tufts in Boston, developed a rating scale that measures the antioxidant content of various plant foods. The scale is called ORAC, short for Oxygen Radical Absorbance Capacity. They discovered that a small group of "super foods" have up to twenty times the antioxidant power of other foods.

Even more amazing, these foods provide more antioxidant power than mega-doses of vitamin supplements! In studies with animals, those that were fed high-ORAC foods had lower biological ages as measured by memory, balance, and capillary strength. "If these findings are borne out in further research, young and middle-aged people may be able to reduce risk of diseases of aging (including senility) simply by adding high-ORAC foods to their diets," said ARS Administrator Floyd P. Horn.

Top-Scoring* Fruits and Vegetables

ORAC units per 100 grams (about 3½ ounces)

Fruits		Vegetables	
Prunes	5770	Kale	1770
Raisins	2830	Spinach	1260
Blueberries	2400	Brussels sprouts	980
Blackberries	2036	Alfalfa sprouts	930
Strawberries	1540	Broccoli flowers	890
Raspberries	1220	Beets	840
Plums	949	Red bell pepper	710
Oranges	750	Onion	450
Red grapes	739	Corn	400
Cherries	670	Eggplant	390
Kiwi fruit	602		
Grapefruit, pink	483		

Agricultural Research Service, USDA, February 8, 1999

Please note: fully two thirds of the highest antioxidant foods on the chart above are fruit.

It is recommended that one eat foods containing at least 3,000 ORAC units a day, which is not difficult, since ½ cup of blueberries contain 2,400 units. So mix it up and eat some berries, prunes or raisins every day and you will easily have over 3,000 units.

* Some fruit less well-known to Americans have been found to have even higher values i.e. Ningxia wolfberries (see p. 67) and pomegranates.

F.Y.I. Organic and sustainably grown foods were found to have significantly higher amounts of antioxidants than conventionally grown food, in an article in the *Journal of Agricultural Food Chemistry*, February 26, 2003;51(5):1237-41, per the website www.mercola.com. On January 26, 2005, the Organic Center Report also indicated that organic foods have elevated antioxidant levels (www.organic-center.org/).

Care and Handling of Fresh Berries

Wild black raspberries

As you can see from the ORAC chart, berries are rich sources of antioxidants, in addition to their fiber, vitamins and minerals, including iron, and as yet unidentified phytonutrients; enjoy them trusting that your body and taste buds know it all already!

I prefer to buy organically grown strawberries and blueberries direct from the local growers (*U-Pick* will insure the freshest fruit) and to forage in the hedgerows for mulberries, raspberries, blackberries and elderberries, which present themselves in this order. They are not usually sprayed and you know that they are fresh.

Berries are fragile. To avoid mold, eat berries within a day or two of harvest. If your only choice is supermarket fare, buy local and in season. Store small quantities of fresh berries in the fridge in well-ventilated containers. Wash quickly, under running water, just before eating to retain nutrients and to discourage mold.

Unfortunately, the berry season is short so you will need to put some up if you want to keep enjoying them throughout the year. I usually forego making jams and jellies and take the lazy way out by freezing or drying them. Frozen berries are most versatile, lending themselves to pancakes, muffins, sauces and shakes, etc. Dry berries are about six times as rich as fresh or frozen ones. I like the blander tasting berries like elderberries and mulberries better this way because their sugars and flavors are more concentrated when dehydrated.

Wash, drain and freeze berries on cookie sheets and then transfer to plastic self-locking bags. Or dry your berries in a dehydrator or on nylon mesh screens in a warm oven with the door propped open a little with a spoon. They are done when they are pliable but not juicy when squeezed.

Fresh blackberries with mango, *Chia Gel* and *Almond Cream*

Fruit Types and Food Combining

The following classification of fruits into *Acid*, *Sub-acid* and *Sweet*, refers to taste qualities and not to acid/alkaline effects, for most fruits are *alkaline-forming*—even citrus! This is presented not to make you go nuts trying to properly combine your food, but for your information and to give you some general guidelines, when you are choosing your breakfast combinations.

The acid fruits do not combine (digest) well with the sweet fruits, but, separately, both combine well with the sub-acid fruits. **Melons** are in their own category because they digest more quickly than other fruits and therefore are best eaten alone (see the end of this chapter). The following chart is based upon *Food Combining Simplified*, by Dennis Nelson.

Acid	Sub-Acid	Sweet
Grapefruit	Apple	Banana*
Kiwi	Apricot	Dates
Kumquat	Berries	Dried Fruits
Lemon	Cherimoya	Fresh Figs
Lime*	Cherries	Muscat Grapes
Orange	Most Grapes	Thompson Grapes
Pineapple	Mango	Papaya
Pomegranate	Nectarine	Persimmon
Strawberry	Peach	Sapote
Tomato**	Pear*	
	Plum	

An illustrated *Food Combining Chart* is available from www.nelsonbooks.com.

While fruit is said to digest best when eaten by itself as an entire meal, this would provide too much sugar and not enough staying power for most people. Fruits combine fairly well with nuts and seeds, especially when the nuts or seeds are presoaked in water to improve their digestibility. Pre-soaking bran and grains will also make them more compatible with fruits.

* These fruit contain little if any salicylates. See box on the following page.

**Tomatoes and avocados (not on the chart), though technically fruits, combine best as follows: tomatoes are best with low starch vegetables, avocados or nuts; avocados are fair with acid fruits, but do not combine well with sweet fruits or proteins (avocados do combine well with vegetables and starches).

Fruit Salads and Smoothies

Use the food combining chart on the opposite page to create luscious fruit salads and smoothies. Keep it simple for best digestion. Use 2 to 3 fruits with contrasting colors and textures. Include berries often and/or plumped fruits. Use about 1 part sweet or acid fruit to 2 parts sub-acid fruit to minimize sugars and fruit acids. Add presoaked nuts and seeds for crunch and to gain nutrients and holding power. (See the box on p. 76 for directions.)

Fruit also combines well with a small amount of cultured vegetable like sauerkraut (or cultured dairy like yogurt or kefir, if tolerated), and can provide even greater regularity when eaten this way. The combination works because the culturing process predigests the veggies so they become more compatible with fruit. Grating apples makes them easier to digest, also. Here is an example:

Apple/Kraut Salad
Serves 1

1 grated apple
2 Tbsp. to ¼ c. sauerkraut
1 tsp. to 1 Tbsp. flaxseed oil

Combine apple and sauerkraut in a serving bowl and sprinkle the top with oil. Serve with a small handful of nuts or seeds.

Salicylates in Foods

Salicylates are naturally occurring, aspirin-like chemicals, usually found under the skin of fruits and veggies, that cause reactions in susceptible individuals. Dr. Benjamin Feingold, an early researcher and advocate for dietary intervention for the treatment of learning disabilities and ADHD, found that many people are reactive to salicylates. Foods that contain negligible amounts are: limes, peeled pears and bananas, most grains, poppy seeds, meats, fish, poultry, dairy and eggs, per researcher Sharla Race. For an extensive list and other resources for food allergies and intolerances visit her website at www.foodcanmakeyouill.co.uk, and for studies supporting diet therapy visit www.feingold.org.

Preparing the *Treasure* chest

These are always a hit with kids. They are pleasing to the eye and palate and fun to eat.

Treasure Apples

Wash apples. Starting from the stem end, using the wide end of a melon baller, scoop out the core--save the first scoop from each to use as the lid to cover the "treasure."

Stuff the apples with raw nut or seed butter or *Nut Cream*, leaving a little headspace for the "lids" to fit back on. Your treasure apples are ready to roll.

Variation: For more hidden treasure, stir currants, raisins and/or sunflower seeds into the nut butter before stuffing.

Melons

Melons are "cucurbits"--in the cucumber family. They are signature fruits of summer and everyone knows how easy and succulently refreshing they are. They express the *yin/yang* of the season—while the weather is hot and dry, they are cooling and rehydrating.

Melons are quickly and easily digested (20 to 30 minutes)* and are better served alone or with raw fruit. Cantaloupe and muskmelon are packed with beta carotene, which is protective to your mucus membranes and helps you to resist colds and allergic reactions, if your body can convert it to vitamin A. Thyroid and/or liver problems can interfere with this conversion.

Cantaloupes and muskmelons are ripe when the color between the webbing is light and the stem slips off leaving a round dimpled scar. Watermelons are ripe when they have a hollow sound—they say *bonk*, not *bink* when tapped with the knuckles. Melons do not ripen after picking so be sure that you choose ripe ones.

Scrub the outside of melons and rinse before cutting to prevent contamination of the flesh by soil bacteria and organisms. Melons spoil quickly once cut so refrigerate leftovers and eat in a day or two.

The seeds and pulp are actually more nourishing than the flesh, as you will learn in the next chapter. Be sure to save them to make the delicious drinks on pp. 91-93. Also see p. 94, suggestions for using watermelon seeds.

Some Melon Types

Canary	Honeydew
Cantaloupe	Muskmelon
Casaba	Persian
Christmas	Watermelon
Crenshaw	

---

* This is why eating that picnic watermelon for dessert can leave you feeling kind of yucky. Eat the watermelon as a between meal snack or as an appetizer and take a walk or play for awhile before the main meal.

Cut pineapple critter with dried cranberry "eyes".

Pineapple

Pineapple is the most popular tropical fruit in the U.S., after bananas. It is sweet tasting but low in calorie and high in vitamin C—15 mg. in ⅔ c. diced (from *The Wellness Encyclopedia of Food and Nutrition*). While most pineapples consumed here have been canned or juiced, the real flavor and benefits from pineapple can only be gotten from consuming it fresh. Like melons, once the fruit has been harvested it will not get any sweeter. It can be stored for a day or two at room temperature to soften, then it will need to be refrigerated.

Though in the category of acid fruit, pineapple is quite alkaline-forming. When eaten raw*, on an empty stomach it is also anti-inflammatory due to its protein digesting enzyme bromelain. This enzyme is the reason that raw pineapple cannot be used to make gelatin—it will digest the protein bonds responsible for gelling. The fresh juice is used in tenderizing marinades for meats and poultry for the same reason.

* Be sure to rinse your mouth out with water or brush your teeth after eating raw pineapple for its fruit acids are strong enough to etch the teeth.

Chapter 3

Plumping Dried Fruit

Plumped Black Mission Figs

Plumping Dried Fruit

Fruit is dried to preserve it. Dried fruit has a higher concentration of natural sugars than fresh fruit because the water, which dilutes the sugars, has been removed. When provided water, dried fruit will return to its natural plump, juicy state, with some textural changes and nutrient losses, notably vitamin C*.

Dried fruit can be hard on the teeth and can upset blood sugar and acid/alkaline balance because of the concentrated sugars. Despite its high fiber content it can cause constipation, if consumed without adequate liquid intake, because it will absorb moisture from the bowel, with the effect of drying it out. Plumping (reconstituting) dried fruit with pure water dilutes its sweetness and makes it moisturizing to the bowel.

If fruit is to be pureed and baked, as in a muffin or waffle recipe, use *Method 1* or *2*. If the fruit is preferred uncooked, as in these *fruit and fiber breakfast* recipes, you might want to use one of the *Mould, Yeast and Bacteria Inhibitors* on p. 72. Those with compromised immunity or digestive problems* might use *Method 3* to kill parasites and their eggs which can adhere to the fruit. After fruit has cooled, one of the inhibitors can be added.

Sulphured Fruit

Sulphured fruit has been treated with, sulphur dioxide. Though it is considered safe by the FDA, this chemical compound can cause serious allergic reactions, particularly in asthmatics.

Sulphur will preserve bright color and enable fruits to be dried with a greater water content. By comparison, unsulphured fruit is darker, drier, sweeter.

Nutritionally, sulphur spares vitamin C, which is usually lost to oxidation, while it destroys other vitamins in the body and may cause other damage. Sulphur is also acid-forming.

* It might be necessary for some to completely avoid dried and reconstituted fruit, at least for awhile, because of their high sugar concentrations and the likelihood of some molds, yeasts and parasites on them.

Wolfberries—an Antioxidant Heavy Weight!

Use plumped wolfberries in smoothies, fruit salads and cereals.

Chinese Wolfberries (*Fructus lycii*)

Chinese name *Gou Qi Zi*, "Goji berries." In Traditional Chinese Medicine these berries are considered tonic in nature. They are high in protein, chromium and antioxidants and are often used to treat impotence, menopausal problems and diabetes. They have a reputation for brightening vision and are used in the treatment of myriad eye problems like glaucoma and cataracts. You can order high quality, whole dried wolfberries from *Crimson Dragon Herbs Co.* (see **Appendix 2**).

F.Y.I. Dr. Gary Young, founder of Young Living Essential Oils, promotes the *Ningxia* species of these berries (*Lycium barbarum*) as the food highest in antioxidants and uses them in several YLEO products. More information can be found in *The Essential Oils Desk Reference* or visit the website www.youngliving.com.

Plumping Methods

First, check fruit for debris and other irregularities. Wash pieces under running water, if necessary. Discard poor quality fruit. The proportion of water to fruit is about 1:1, depending on the size of the fruit. Smaller fruit like raisins, currants or dried berries require about 1½:1.

Because of the acids* in fruit, I recommend to soak, cook and otherwise process it in china, glass or enamelware. Avoid tin, copper, silver and aluminum containers and utensils. Ceramics should have food safe glazes.

Method 1—Overnight (Raw)

Fill a pint jar to within ½" of a the top with loosely packed, pitted fruit – approximately 1½ cups. Fill the jar again, this time right to the top, with pure water – approximately 1¼ cups. Loosely affix a lid to the jar, or in some way cover, and let stand to soak at room temperature for 6 to 8 hours, or overnight.

In hot weather, prevent fermentation by soaking in the refrigerator, with lid firmly affixed, to prevent spillage. This yields about 2 cups, whole plumped fruit.

Method 2 —Quick

To quickly reconstitute fruit, combine with equal part boiling water, in a jar or glass bowl. Cover tightly and let stand for 20 to 30 minutes.

Method 3—Traditional (Cooked)

Combine fruit and the desired proportion of water in a glass pot. Cover, bring to a boil and remove from heat or simmer for a few minutes. Keep the cover on and allow to cool before storing in the refrigerator or blending. Cooked fruit and purees and sauces made from it, combine better with cooked cereals, pancakes and waffles than raw fruit. Cooking fruit raises its glycemic index.

---

* Though fruits contain acids they are generally alkaline-forming in the body. Exceptions include plums/prunes and cranberries.

Easy and Elegant Fruit Syrups

Always save the sweet soak water from plumped fruits to serve over fresh fruit, pancakes and waffles, for pureeing fruits, to stir into tea, and to add to smoothies and other recipes instead of fruit juice or other less nutritious sweeteners. You will find many ways to enjoy this rich "liquor."

Sliced Kiwi with *Figgy Syrup*

Fruit syrups are the simplest things to make. You will find lots of ways to use them. By using only enough water to cover the fruit by about one finger joint, the syrup should have plenty of body without having to boil it to reduce further.

Figgy Syrup

After figs have been plumped, use some of the sweet soak water as a syrup over fresh fruit slices, cereal, pancakes or waffles.

Plumped Fruit Purees

Apricots, dates, prunes and figs make especially tasty purees. Combine in the blender: plumped pitted fruit and soaking or cooking water (the proportions given above will work in a standard size home blender).

Blend with a stop/start action. Stop blender to release air bubbles when action ceases. Add more water if needed for blender to work.

These purees are thick and can be thinned with extra water, fruit juice or vegetable broth to the consistency desired. Store in the refrigerator. Use them to sweeten smoothies, as a binder in gluten-free recipes and in place of jams and jellies. For a refreshingly delicious and even healthier sauce or spread, combine fruit puree half and half with *Chia Gel* (p. 117).

Apricot Sauce *(Method #3)*

Yields about a pint

Combine in a small saucepan, cover bring to a boil, then turn down to simmer for 5 to 10 minutes:

2 c. unsulfured apricots (pitted)
2 c. water
1-3" cinnamon stick (optional)

Remove from the heat and let stand to cool (covered). Remove the cinnamon stick* and blend apricots and liquid in the blender until creamy. Add a little more water for blending or desired consistency. Use as a smoothie ingredient or as a topping for pancakes, ice cream, etc.

---

* Leave the cinnamon stick out at room temperature for a day or 2 to air dry. It may be used several more times.

Figs are high in fiber, silica (for hair, skin, teeth and nails), iron, folic acid, calcium, potassium, B₁, B₂ and niacin. Their tiny seeds are anti-parasitic. Figs and prunes are highly beneficial for all blood types, per Dr. Peter D'Adamo.

Fig Sauce *(Method #1)*

Yields 2 cups (1 pint)

2 c. Black Mission figs
2 c. water

Soak figs in water in a jar or covered bowl overnight, or for 8 hrs. Add one of the "Inhibitors" above.

Using a blender or food processor, make a puree of the figs and soak water. Add a little more water if it needs to be thinned. That's all! Use as a spread, filling, topping for ice cream, sweetener for hot cereal or as a smoothie ingredient. Thin a little more, or combine with equal parts *Chia Gel*, to make a sauce to serve with pancakes or waffles.

Kernels 'n Cores

Small amounts of apple and pear seeds, and apricot, plum (prune), nectarine and peach kernels may be eaten and are beneficial. In addition to proteins and minerals e.g. iron and silica, they, like almonds, contain B_{17}, a vitamin that some studies have shown to have anti-tumor activity. Use only 2 to 3 kernels or the seeds of 1 or 2 apples daily, for they also contain a trace of cyanide and would be toxic if eaten in large quantities.

Decorticated apricot kernels have had the toxic apex removed. They are delicious and may be used freely instead of nuts and other seeds as snacks and to add crunch to other foods. They are available from *Crimson Dragon Herbs Co.* (see **Appendix 2**). They make an excellent trail mix when combined with wolfberries, from the same supplier.

Mold, Yeast and Bacteria Inhibitors

Use 3 to 5 drops of grapefruit seed extract or ½ tsp. citric acid crystals per pint, in any method to kill yeasts, mold and bacteria that are common in dried fruits.

Some Mildly Sweet Dried Fruit:

Elderberries	Wolfberries
Mulberries	Jujube (red) dates

These are a welcomed change from the more commonly used raisins or dates pieces. They may be plumped for *fruit and fiber breakfasts* or to add to hot cereals.

See also, *Using Plumped Fruit in Smoothies* on p. 99.

Chapter 4

Amazing Nuts and Seeds

Homemade *Almond Milk*

Amazing Nuts and Seeds

Nuts, the large seeds of tree fruit, and smaller seeds have been part of Man's diet from the time we first began to forage for our food. This is not surprising for nuts derive from 8 to 18% of their calories from protein, while seeds are even higher with 11 to 25%*. And even today, oils pressed from nuts and seeds are among the most widely used plant products in the world.

Nuts and seeds have gone through their cycle of defamation, like the much maligned egg, which fell to the blows of the "fat gestapo" when cholesterol, and fats in general, were being single-mindedly blamed for heart disease**. Now we know better and new science is discovering previously unknown nutrients in nuts and seeds, like the beneficial essential fatty acids in almonds, walnuts, macadamia nuts, chia and flax seeds. Even the 5 o'clock TV news is touting "22 almonds per day will lower cholesterol."

So, if you have been feeling guilty about eating nuts and seeds, relax. Additionally, presoaking them in water releases their life force and reduces and enhances their fats:

> ➢ Some fats are burned up in the process of "respiration"
> ➢ enzymes that digest the fats are created within the nuts/seeds

Additionally, some vegetarians, especially those with O Blood Type, might have a higher need for fats and proteins in their diet. Nuts and seeds fit the bill adding flavor, versatility and cloying power.

For the dairy sensitive, nuts and seeds offer minerals. Even when the soil is deficient, Mother Nature makes sure that the correct concentration of key nutrients are packed into the nuts and seeds for they carry the blueprint and the survival pack needed for the germination and beginning of growth of a new generation.

---

* *The Wellness Encyclopedia of Food and Nutrition.*

**See *Nourishing Traditions*, by Sally Fallon for more about the benefits of fats in traditional human diets.

Some Often Overlooked Facts

The various nuts and seeds are veritable powerhouses of other nutrients as well, including B-complex vitamins and minerals. But before everyone runs out to stock up, there are some things we need to know:

1) Most nuts and seeds need to be refrigerated to prevent rancidity.

2) Most commercially sold products have been roasted (actually deep fried) at high temperatures which saturate, and may even damage, naturally unsaturated fats. They may also contain as much as 10 calories more per ounce (per *The Wellness Encyclopedia of Food and Nutrition*).

3) While it is best to purchase nuts raw, one should not consume many raw nuts because they contain powerful enzyme inhibitors* that can interfere with digestion.

4) Persons who are infected with the herpes virus may need to forgo most nuts because of their high arginine** content.

Storage and Care of Nuts and Seeds

Shells protect nuts and seeds from light, heat, moisture and air. For this reason unshelled nuts and seeds store better than shelled. Shelled nuts and seeds may be refrigerated in tight containers for a few months. Nuts may be frozen in vapor proof bags or containers for up to 2 years; seeds for a year or more. Canned nuts will keep 1 year. **Note:** Shelled almonds and filberts are the most stable nuts and can be stored at room temperature for several weeks or months.

When purchasing shelled, raw nuts and seeds look for ones that are whole, and evenly colored, preferably sold from a refrigerator case or from bulk bins where the turn over is high. Avoid if the flesh appears yellow or brown. Some, like Diamond™ walnuts, are nitrogen packed in cans or bags to prevent rancidity.

---

* See how to deactivate enzyme inhibitors on the next page. For more fascinating information read the the classic, *Enzyme Nutrition*, by Dr. Edward Howell.

**Chestnuts, hickory nuts and coconuts contain the least amount of arginine, per *Nutrition Almanac, Fifth Edition*, by Lavon J. Dunne (2002).

How to Get the Most from Nuts and Seeds

In addition to proteins, heart healthy essential fatty acids, B-complex vitamins and minerals, nuts and seeds contain DNA—the genetic blueprint! If presoaked in water before eating the *life force* is engaged and they undergo amazing changes in flavor and texture: they expand slightly and become sweeter, crisper, more digestible and rich sources of enzymes—metabolic facilitators.

Presoaking is my preferred way of handling nuts and seeds. Raw nuts contain powerful *enzyme inhibitors* that can block digestion, while all seeds (including grains) contain *phytic acid* (*phytates*) in their surface skins, that bind with minerals making them difficult to utilize. Presoaking rids them of both. Additionally, when nuts and seeds are presoaked, they develop the enzymes to digest their own fats!

While roasting will deactivate enzyme inhibitors, it leaves phytates intact and the high temperatures that commercial roasters use damages fats and saturates them*. When you want the flavor and texture that roasting gives, roast in *no higher* than a 250° F. oven. 30 minutes is enough for most nuts and seeds. Still, roasted nuts and seeds are not as beneficial because they lack the enzyme activity of presoaked nuts and seeds thus are more difficult to digest.

Presoaking and Storing Nuts and Seeds

Use about twice the volume of plain water and soak for 8 to 12 hours. ¼ tsp. citric acid can be added to a pint of soak water to inhibit molds. Drain and rinse in a colander or mesh strainer, then proceed with directions for making *Basic Nut Milk* (p. 80). For eating whole, drain for several minutes, or lay on a clean towel to blot excess moisture. Store in a loosely covered container in the refrigerator.

Whole nuts and seeds can be safely stored for a couple of days this way, so soak only what you'll be able to use. They make handy nutritious snacks and will add crunch and staying power to fruit meals.

---

* Damaged and rancid fats are carcinogenic. Nuts and seeds roasted at too high a temperature will develop a bitter flavor and a greasy texture.

Calcium without Dairy Products

While celebrities don milk moustaches, dairy allergies, both known and unknown, abound. The dairy industry spends a mint to entice you to *drink* and *eat* your milk. But what is glamorous about sinus congestion, respiratory and/or ear infections, G.I. problems or arthritis? And this is just the tip of the iceberg for persons who are dairy sensitive or intolerant. Foods that are truly beneficial for us get no hype because they are unprocessed and there is little profit to be made by middlemen.

A common concern is *if we eliminate dairy products, where will we get our calcium?* And it is not just calcium, but a whole symphony of minerals and vitamins that make our bones and teeth strong and healthy. Elephants do not consume dairy products so how do they grow to be so big and strong? After they are weaned, *they eat their greenies*! We can get our minerals from greens, too, but we also have access to sea vegetables, nuts and seeds and mineral rich bones (e.g. from canned salmon and sardines). While dairy milk contains too much protein and phosphorus to be either alkalizing or a good source of calcium*, almonds are rich in both calcium and the magnesium needed to metabolize it.

Nutrients and Qualities of Various Nuts and Seeds

Almonds are a good source of vitamins A and E and calcium, magnesium and potassium, as well as essential fatty acids. The skins contain anti-parasitic tannins. Unlike most other nuts and seeds, shelled almonds are stable at room temperature. (They may be blanched to remove the skins before making into milk.)

Brazil nuts are high in the mineral selenium—about 80 mcg. of this healthful antioxidant per nut. They make an excellent cream or pudding.

Filberts (hazelnuts) are high in Vitamins A and E and calcium, magnesium and potassium. (They, like almonds, may be stored at room temperature for several months.)

---

* **Note:** The countries that eat the most dairy also have the highest osteoporosis—perhaps because these countries also eat the most of everything, but also because the minerals in pasteurized milk are difficult to absorb due to the absence of phosphatase, an enzyme destroyed by heating. See *Total Health*, by Dr. Joseph Mercola.

Macadamia nuts are high in total fat, including a generous portion of Omega-3's. If you can find raw, they make a white, mild tasting milk.

Pecans are rich in essential fatty acids and potassium. They make a beige colored, mild tasting milk.

Pumpkin*, squash and melon seeds are good sources of B vitamins, protein and zinc. Pumpkin seeds are anti-parasitic and specific for pin-worms. Seeds may be blended with hulls intact and strained before serving (see recipes on pp. 91-93).

Sesame seeds* are high richest in calcium and quite high in niacin, potassium and zinc. The unhulled seeds may be stored at room temperature. Milk made from the hulled seeds is lower in calcium but milder tasting. 1 Tbsp. of tahini (sesame paste) contains 64 mg. of calcium, per *Nutrition Almanac.*

Sunflower seeds* are high in B vitamins, vitamin E and potassium. Their milk has a unique flavor and grey/tan color. Add a tablespoon of lemon juice to a quart of sunflower seed milk to prevent discoloration from oxidation.

Walnuts are rich in Omega-3 heart healthy essential fatty acids. They make a white, mild tasting milk.

Cashews are not nuts at all but the blossom end of a fruit in the poison ivy family, for this reason persons who are sensitive to poison ivy should avoid eating these raw or drinking milk made from raw cashews. Cashews (along with peanuts) are the highest in saturated fats. Roasting cashews seems to de-activate the sensitizing components. (Cashews are not recommended for any blood-type, per D'Adamo.)

---

* These milks might taste stronger than most other nut and seed milks so you might want to sweeten a little by replacing 1 cup of water with fruit juice or by adding a little honey, or maple or agave syrup (see **Appendix 1** for nutritional information and **Appendix 2** for sources).

A Comparison of Calcium and Magnesium in Nuts and Seeds

Nut or Seed (1 cup unless noted)	Calcium (mg)	Magnesium (mg)
Almonds	332	386
Brazil nuts	260	351
Cashews	53	374
Chestnuts/oz.	5.4	8.5
Coconut	10	37
Hazelnuts	282	313
Hickory/5 nuts	9	24
Macadamia nuts	94	155
Pecans	79	142
Pine nuts/oz.	3	66
Pistachios	173	203
Pumpkin and squash seeds	71	738
Sesame seeds	1404*	270
Sunflower seeds	174	57
Tahini/Tbsp.	64	14
Walnuts	99	131

Data for this chart was taken from *Nutrition Almanac, Fifth Edition,*
by Lavon J. Dunne, 2001

Note: Peanuts are not on the chart above because they are legumes and require different preparation to make them digestible.

* About half of the calcium in sesame seeds is bound to oxalate and be unavailable to the body, per *The Wellness Encyclopedia of Food and Nutrition.*

Nut Milks

Soy, rice, almond and even oat milks are gaining more popularity in the health-conscious market, but my feeling is that homemade nut milks are better in every way. They are the freshest, have the least number of ingredients, do not need sweeteners and other additives and have not been processed with heat; therefore they contain live enzymes. And they do pass the taste test! With ¾ to 1 cup of nuts or seeds yielding a quart of milk, homemade is also cost effective.

This milk is best suited for use on cereals, in smoothies, or in baked goods or breads because it can be a little grainy. Longer blending will give a finer texture. If you want to use it as a plain beverage, strain through a fine mesh strainer or several layers of cheese cloth.

Basic Nut Milk

Yields 1 quart

¾ c. hulled, raw nuts (or seeds)
2 c. water (for pre-soaking—this water will be discarded)
3+ c. water

Combine nuts with 2 cups of water in a jar or bowl and let stand for 4 to 8 hours, or overnight (almonds are very dense and need 24 hours). **Option:** Add ¼ tsp. citric acid crystals to kill molds.

In the morning, drain and rinse in a colander and combine in the blender with ¾ cup fresh water. Blend until you have a smooth, creamy consistency, adding a little more water if necessary for good blender action. Blend for about a minute, or up to 2 minutes for a finer texture.

Add remaining water to make a quart, then blend again briefly. Pour into a quart glass jar and skim the foam off, or let stand for a couple of minutes to let the foam settle, then fill to the top with more water. Affix an enameled lid with rubber gasket—canning jars and lids work great— then store in the refrigerator. Nut milk keeps for up to 5 days. Shake before using. **Note:** 5 to 10 drops of stabilized oxygen may be added per pint to extend shelf life.

Variations: While the nuts have already become sweeter due to the pre-soaking process, to sweeten more you may replace 1 cup of water with a cup of fruit juice, or add 1 Tbsp. maple or agave syrup, and/or 1 to 2 tsp. vanilla, almond or other glycerite (alcohol-free).

Tips: Extend shelf life by returning the remainder of the milk to the refrigerator immediately after pouring. 5 to 10 drops of stabilized oxygen O_7 may also be added per quart to kill bacteria that can cause fermentation and an "off" flavor. See *Aerobic Industries* in **Appendix 2**.

My favorite nut milks are walnut, almond and pecan. Try them all or check out *Eat Right 4 Your Type*, by Peter D'Adamo, N.D., and find out which ones are recommended for your blood type.

Basic Nut Cream

Yields about 1½ cups

¾ c. hulled, raw nuts (or seeds)
2 c. water (for pre-soaking—this water will be discarded)
¾ to 1 c. water

Combine nuts with water in a jar or bowl and let stand for 4 to 8 hours, or overnight (almonds are very dense and need 24 hours).

In the morning, drain and rinse in a colander and combine in the blender with ¾ cup fresh water. Blend until you have a smooth, creamy consistency, adding a little more water if necessary for good blender action. Blend for a minute or longer for a finer texture.

Taste and sweeten, if you like with a little raw honey and blend briefly; the presoak process has already converted some of the starches into sugars so sweetening may not be necessary. Sometimes I add a teaspoon of lemon juice and/or a little vanilla or almond glycerite.

A Comparison between Homemade and Commercial Almond Milk

Volume= 8 fluid ounces

Nutrient	Homemade^	Commercial*
Calories	176.7	60
Total Carbs (g.)	5.2	8
Sugar (g.)	None added	7
Dietary fiber	3.2	<1
Calcium (mg.)	64.8	20% DV (200)
Magnesium (mg.)	70.9	NA
Potassium (mg.)	205.9	180
Total Fat (g.) ♥	14.4♥	2.5♥
Saturated (g.)	1.2	0
Cholesterol (mg.)	0	0
Protein (g.)	4.9	1
Vitamin E (I.U.)	10.5	50% DV (30)
Iron (mg.)	1.3	2% DV (.36)
Vitamin A (I.U.)	2.6	20% DV (1,000)
Vitamin D (I.U.)	NA	25% DV (100)
Cost per cup	$.28**	$.67
Cost per quart	$1.13**	$2.69

^ The figures for homemade almond milk are based upon data from *Nutrition Almanac, Fifth Edition*, by Lavon J. Dunne.

* Almond Breeze "Original" almond milk (non-organic), produced by *Blue Diamond Growers' Co-op*™; data is per package. www.bluediamond.com

NA-- not available

DV—Daily Values. Numbers in parentheses are my computations.

♥ 7% Saturated / 48% Monounsaturated / 16% Polyunsaturated (per *Wellness A-Z*, published by UC Berkeley, 2002).

**This is based on a cost of $3.99/pound for non-organic almonds.

Comments—

The homemade almond milk is higher in fat and calories because, judging from the protein content, more almonds were used to make it. The fat is 48% cholesterol lowering monounsaturated fatty acids.

The ingredients in the homemade almond milk are: distilled water and almonds.

The ingredients in the commercial almond milk are: purified water, evaporated cane juice, almonds, tricalcium phosphate, sea salt, potassium citrate, carageenan, soy lecithin, d-alpha-tocopherol (natural vitamin E), vitamin A palmitate, vitamin D_2.

Because the commercial milk is made with fewer almonds, it needs a thickener (carageenan) to give it body and mineral supplementation to boost its nutrients. The homemade milk contains beneficial live enzymes while the commercial has been heated and may contain chemicals leached from the inner lining of the package.

Homemade almond milk (left) compared to commercial.

Making Almond Milk

Popping the skins off blanched almonds is often a job that kids like to do.
Pop them off in a bowl of water so that the almonds won't fly all over the kitchen.
(*Shucks, Mom, you're no fun!*)

Almond Milk (see photo on the previous page)

Yields 1 quart

¾ c. raw almonds (4½ oz.)
Water for presoaking
¾ c. water for initial blending
More water

Soak almonds in twice as much water for 24 hours. Drain and rinse. Blend with water just to the top of nuts, for about 2 minutes or until you have a smooth cream. Add enough more water to fill a quart jar. Use on cereals, for smoothies and other recipes that call for milk. Store in the refrigerator.

Blanching Almonds

Almond skins contain anti-parasitic tannins and provide fiber and minerals, but you or your family might prefer the milk to be pure white, rather than flecked with brown, if so, either blanch to remove skins before blending or pour blended milk through a fine mesh strainer or several layers of cheesecloth. To blanch almonds, place in very hot water for 1 minute. Drain and rinse. Cover again with cold water. Pop the skins off.

Walnut Milk (follow *Basic Nut Milk* directions)

Walnut Milk is the easiest to make. Walnuts only need overnight soaking and there are no coarse skins to remove. The flavor of the milk is mild and it has a smooth texture and a nice white color, which is appealing. In addition, walnuts are a good source of essential heart healthy fatty acids and vitamin E. They are beneficial for all blood types (except Type B, secretor, for whom they are neutral), whereas almonds are neutral for all blood types, per Dr. Peter D'Adamo, *Live Right 4 Your Type.*

Note: Choose walnut halves rather than pieces for the smaller pieces go rancid faster. Look for nuts with whitish to light beige flesh rather than yellow or brown, for the fats in the latter have spoiled. If possible, buy walnuts from refrigerated stock.

Coconuts—Don't Knock 'Em

Coconut used to be a bad baddie, but now it appears to be a good goodie, at least for some people*! The raw flesh is alkaline-forming and the sweet water** is rich in enzymes. The flesh has always gotten a bad rap for its high saturated fat content, but it also contains healthier fats that increase metabolism and strengthen the immune system!

Coconut oil is 60% medium chain triglycerides (MCT) which are burned as carbohydrates, not stored as fat. This is good news for athletes because it spares glucose. It's also good news for dieters and diabetics because it helps to balance blood sugar.

Coconut oil also contains caprylic and lauric acids which are immune supportive and help to fight *Candida* yeast overgrowth and Epstein-Barr Virus. It can be taken alone, as a supplement, or eaten with other foods instead of butter or other fats. (Be sure to include a variety of fat sources in your diet—including omega-3's—to have a good balance of fatty acids.)

Udo Erasmus, oil expert and author of *Fats that Heal, Fats that Kill*, feels that the best way to consume coconut fat is with the flesh. It's better for the cardiovascular system this way and won't cause weight gain.

Usually a whole fresh coconut is more than a family of four will eat up in a few days, so I cut it into chunks, wrap and freeze for later use. Except for a little textural change, it is as good as fresh.

I keep unsulphured, unsweetened, desiccated coconut on hand, also, for breakfasts and snacks. It's great on fruit salads. To lightly toast, spread on a cookie sheet and bake in a 225°F. pre-heated oven for 20 to 25 minutes.

For Cooking: Coconut oil has a high smoke point and therefore is not damaged by high heat as are most other oils. It is perfect for greasing the skillet or waffle iron. Melt a small amount and spread with a wide pastry brush.

*Not everyone agrees that coconuts are beneficial, per Dr. Peter D'Adamo (*Live Right 4 Your Type*), coconuts should be avoided by all blood types except Type O, non-secretors, for whom it is neutral.

**Donna Gates, author of *The Body Ecology Diet*, has pioneered the making of "Coconut Water Kefir". You can visit her website at www.bodyecologydiet.com for instructions.

The following is one of my favorite beverages. It should be sweet and almost clear. One nut can yield up to a cup! Taken on an empty stomach this can be quite healing.

Fresh Coconut Water

Serves 1

Choose a heavy nut with an uncracked, unblemished shell—it should slosh when shaken. Bore a hole through the softest "eye" with a clean screw-driver or ice pick. Drain the water into a glass or measuring cup. Strain out any debris from the shell. Drink immediately for the beneficial enzymes.

Use only pure white coconut flesh for the following recipe—discard any that is yellow or discolored. Refrigerate for up to a week. Add 1 Tbsp. lime juice per 7 ounces for longer storage--up to 3 weeks, per Aajonus Vonderplanitz, author of the Recipe for Living Without Disease, *(2002).*

Fresh* Coconut Milk

Yields 1 to 1½ cups

Blend 1 c. raw grated coconut, or ½ c. small chunks, with 1 c. water for about 2 minutes. Strain through a fine mesh strainer (save the pulp to add fiber and lighten s/cereals, cookies, waffles and muffins). Add more water to yield at least a cup. Store in the refrigerator. Cream will come to the top within a short time. Skim off cream to use plain, or shake before serving. (The cream is smooth and delicious—suitable for use in beverages, or to top fruits and desserts.)

Buying Desiccated Coconut

Unsulphured, unsweetened dried coconut should be purchased from refrigerator cases. It should be pure white, not yellow in color. Store in the refrigerator or freezer in vapor proof jars or bags to prevent rancid-ity. If fresh coconut is not available, try the recipe below.

Coconut Milk from Dried Coconut (Yields 3 cups): soak 1 c. in 4 c. water for 20 minutes or longer. Then blend and strain. Press the residue through cheesecloth or put it through a juicer. The fat that rises to the top will be hard and can be skimmed off or strained out. (The fat can be used in cooking or greasing, per the previous page.)

---

* Commercial coconut milk is usually sold in cans and contains preservatives and thickeners like guar gum, which can be irritating to the gluten-sensitive.

Seed Milks

Sunflower Seed Milk

Yields 1 quart

¾ c. sunflower seeds, hulled
water for presoaking

additional water for blending
2 to 3 tsp. lemon juice

Soak seeds overnight in twice as much water. In the morning drain and rinse and blend with about 1 cup of water until it is creamy, about 1½ minutes. Add lemon juice (to prevent discoloration) and enough additional water to make a quart.

Variation:
To sweeten, replace 1 cup of water with fruit juice, or add 1 to 2 tablespoons of maple syrup, if desired.

Sunny Seed Cream

Yields 1 pint

Presoak 1 cup sunflower seeds in 2 to 3 cups of water for 4 to 8 hours. Drain and rinse seeds and combine in the blender with:

3 oz. thawed pineapple juice concentrate
enough fresh water to just cover the seeds
a pinch of sea salt
1 Tbsp. lemon juice

Blend until creamy. Serve over fruit and/or s/cereal. Enjoy!

Brown, unhulled sesame seeds have more calcium than the white hulled seeds, but the hull contains some oxalic acid, tannins and minerals that give it a bitterness, even after presoaking the seeds. By far the tastiest sesame milk is made from raw hulled seeds, but the easiest is made from tahini (sesame paste) made from hulled or unhulled, raw or roasted seeds. This milk has a silky texture which makes it suitable for drinking

Sesame Milk

Yields 1 cup

1 Tbsp. raw tahini (preferably from raw seeds)
1 c. water

Combine in the blender and process for about 30 seconds. Drink as is or add a little maple syrup or honey, or stir in a tablespoon of *Carob Syrup* (p. 90) for a special treat.

Variation: Other raw nut or seed butters may be substituted for tahini.

Buying and Storing Sunflower, Sesame and Pumpkin Seeds

Buy hulled raw sunflower and sesame seeds from refrigerator cases, if possible. Sunflower seeds should be medium gray, not yellow or brown. Hulled sesame seeds should be off-white. Pumpkin seeds should be green, not yellow or brown. Store them in moisture and vapor-proof containers in the refrigerator or freezer.

Note: Unhulled (brown) sesame seeds need no refrigeration.

Carob is made from the fleshy pod of a leguminous plant, also known as honey locust or St. John's bread. While it is not chocolate, carob can be delicious and satisfying, without the dairy, excito-toxins and oxalic acid. It is high in protein, calcium, potassium, B-vitamins and pectin.

Hot Carob-coa

Makes 2 cups

2 c. of nut or seed milk
1 to 2 Tbsp. Carob Syrup (recipe below)

Strain homemade nut milk through several layers of cheese cloth first, if necessary to remove small granules, then warm over medium heat. Stir in syrup and serve.

Carob Syrup

Makes about 1½ cups

1 c. water
1 c. toasted carob powder
¼ c. raw honey*
¼ tsp. *Fearn*™ Liquid (soya) Lecithin, **or** coconut oil

Stir the carob powder into ½ cup water to make a paste. Then stir in honey and lecithin; now stir in the remaining water. Store in an *easy-to-pour* bottle in the refrigerator. Shake or stir before using.

Use 1 to 2 tablespoons per cup of hot or cold nut or seed milk.

Variation: Replace honey with 6 Tbsp. *rapadura*** and heat mixture over medium heat until sugar is dissolved. Store in fridge. Stir before serving.

* Do not feed honey to children under 2 years of age.

Dehydrated natural sugar cane juice contains the original nutrients. Looks and tastes like brown sugar e.g. *Sucanat*™ (see **Appendix 1).

Making Milks from Seeds and Pulp

Nature offers us more in squash, pumpkins and melons than the starchy/sweet flesh. The seeds are the real treasure within. It is here that Mother Nature has put the most energy, packing these seeds with proteins, essential fatty acids, minerals and B vitamins – even the pulp, the little strings that are attached to the seeds, is more nutritious than the flesh! Here are some some ways to enjoy them without roasting.

The following milk and nog have a richer flavor if made from seeds that have been baked or steamed*. Freeze your seeds and pulp for later use if you cannot make this a day or two after removing from the gourd.

Squash or Pumpkin Seed Milk

Yields 1 quart

Combine in blender:

1 c. winter squash or pumpkin seeds and pulp (raw or cooked)
1 c. water

Blend until texture appears thick and creamy, adding a little more water if necessary for good blender action. Pour this coarse seed milk through a sieve – stainless steel mesh works well. Stir with a wooden pestle to speed the process along. Pour a little more water through milky-looking pulp. Use enough total water to yield 1 qt. seed milk. Discard seed pulp.

Are Your Pumpkin Seeds X-Rated?

Of course, it is easier to make pumpkin seed milk from dried, hulled seeds, but you will be missing out on the nutrients in the pulp. The best tasting seeds come from "naked," or hulless, varieties which should be dark green. Some of these, like *Godiva*, are available to home gardeners. Super nutritious, hulless *Styrian* seeds can be ordered from the Grain and Salt Society (see **Appendix 2**).

---

* Cut squash into chunks and steam or cut in half from stem to blossom end and place cut side down on a cookie sheet for baking. Bake in a 350° F. oven for about 45 minutes or until skin can be pricked with a fork. The seeds and pulp scoop out more easily after cooking also.

Squash Nog made from pumpkin seeds and pulp.

Here is another one of my favorite seed recipes. I enjoy this as a snack, it is so delicious and satisfying!

Squash Nog

Yields 2 to 3 cups

Make the *Squash or Pumpkin Seed Milk* on the previous page but use less water for a thicker consistency. After you have strained it, whisk or stir in the following:

1 to 2 Tbsp. maple syrup or agave syrup*
1 to 2 tsp. vanilla glycerite (alcohol-free extract)
¼ to ½ tsp. nutmeg

* Agave syrup has a low glycemic index and is suitable for diabetics. (See **Appendix 1** for nutritional information and **Appendix 2** for sources).

Melon Seed Drink

While I like it best made fresh, when you have an over abundance of melons, you may freeze surplus seeds and pulp in reclosable plastic bags for later use. Supermarkets that sell cut melon sections will often be happy to give you the seeds!

Melon Seed Drink

Yields 1 pint

Seeds and pulp from 1 ripe melon* (approximately 1 c.)
1 c. water (or ½ c. each water and fruit juice)

Scoop out the seeds from one ripe melon (cantaloupe, muskmelon or Crenshaw, etc.), pulp and all; drop it into the blender, add 1 cup purest water you can get or ½ cup water and ½ cup fruit juice. Blend on low speed for about 30 seconds, then increase speed and blend for about 1 minute. Pour through a fine mesh strainer to remove seed hulls.

* Be sure to scrub and blot the outside of melons before cutting them to prevent the spread of bacteria from the rind to the flesh.

93

Using Watermelon Seeds

Besides being beautiful, delicious and refreshing, watermelon is a gentle diuretic that is cleansing and tonic to the kidneys and bladder. The flesh is full of carotenes, including lycopene—in fact, watermelon is richer in lycopene than tomatoes! The rind and seeds contain proteins. I always prefer the ones with seeds, though the *seedless* varieties do contain immature seeds.

Watermelon seeds may be chewed along with the flesh or blended with the flesh, then strained. Dr. Ann Wigmore used to use watermelon as the base for her summer *Energy Soup* (blended salad). Though this is not food combining "by the book," the other ingredients are raw so it is still easy to digest and delicious.

The seeds may be saved, rinsed and dried for tea*, also. They are diuretic and healing for the bladder and kidneys, especially helpful to promote a normal flow of urine. Cover a teaspoon of seeds with 1 pint of boiling water and steep for 15 to 20 minutes. Sip through the day.

* Watermelon seed tea was mentioned in about 75 of the *Edgar Cayce* readings. It was recommended to drink a little at a time. It is available from the *Heritage Store* (see **Appendix 2**).

Cultured Nuts and Seeds

Cultured foods are predigested and can help to provide the right flora for optimal intestinal health. Some people tolerate these foods well while others do not.

The following is quite easy to make and tastes remarkably like dairy. I have also made it using about a tablespoon of plain yogurt as a starter. Make sure that the carton says that it contains "live culture" and bring it to room temperature before adding. Fermentation works best in a room not warmer than 72°F. In hot weather, check frequently to get the right flavor. Rejuvelac, a fermented grain beverage can be substituted for water and starter (recipe on p. 35).

Almond "Yogurt"
Yields 1 cup

1 c. almonds
¾ c. water
½ packet of *Body Ecology*™ *Starter**

Soak the almonds for 24 hours in 2 cups of pure water (almonds are the densest nuts and require more time than the others). Drain and rinse. Blanch almonds.

Now blend nuts with water, until creamy (about 2 minutes). Add a little more water, a tablespoon at a time, if necessary for good blender action. Stir the starter in last. Pour into a non-metallic (preferably glass) jar or bowl and cover loosely with a clean towel. Let stand at room temperature for 12 hours or more, checking the flavor after 4 to 8 hours to get the degree of fermentation you want. Refrigerate. Serve with fresh fruit salad or stir in pureed fruit. Sweeten if desired.

Variations: use other nuts or seeds instead almonds.

Cheesey Dip or Spread--add a little salt, lemon juice and your favorite spices, or season as follows: stir in ½ tsp. salt and 2 finely chopped scallions. Serve with rye krisps or veggie sticks and wedges of avocado.

* To order by phone, call: 1-866-KEFIR-4U (1-866-533-4748).

Walnut Crème Fraîche

Yields 1 pint

Walnuts are easier to process than almonds because they require only about 8 hours soaking time and they don't need to be blanched.

1 c. walnuts
¾ c. water
1 packet *Body Ecology*™ *Starter* (see previous reference for ordering)
1 tsp. maple syrup (optional)

Soak walnuts overnight in 2 cups of pure water. Drain and rinse. Blend with water until creamy. Add enough extra water to make 2 cups. Stir in starter. Stir in maple syrup.

Pour into a 1 pt. glass bottle (like wide mouth Ball™ canning jar) and firmly affix lid. Let stand for 10 to 12 hours at room temperature or until it tastes tart. Refrigerate. This can be used like regular sour cream, though it is thinner.

The following has a pale green color and a pleasantly smooth texture thanks to the chia seed.

Pumpkin Seed Yogurt or Spread

Yields about 1⅔ cups

1 c. pumpkin seeds (plus 2 c. water for presoak)
1 c. water
1 packet *Body Ecology*™ *Starter*
2 Tbsp. chia seeds (optional)

Presoak pumpkin seeds overnight. Drain and rinse. Blend with water until creamy. Pour into a glass jar or bowl. With a non-metal utensil, stir in starter and chia seeds. Set in a warm place for 4 hours or more until pleasantly fermented. Use as is or stir in one of the following seasonings, if desired: 2 Tbsp. maple syrup or ½ tsp. salt. Refrigerate to hold flavor and slow the fermentation process.

Chapter 5
Smoothies

Strawberry/Pear Smoothie

Smoothies

"Chew your beverages, drink your solids." This advice applies to raw and cooked foods alike. Smoothies slide down so easily that there is a tendency to want to just chug them, but chew because they are blends of nutritionally dense ingredients. In fact, I like to think of smoothies as "assisted solids," that is, the addition of liquid and blending increases surface area and gives salivary enzymes better access to begin the digestive process.* So relax and savor!

By using fresh fruit in season, or frozen berries, and even frozen bananas, and different nuts and seeds for the milk, this high-protein, high-fiber meal or snack can be varied throughout the year. Go for the more deeply colored fruits to access their cornucopia of pigments and phytochemicals. The deeper the color, the more nutrients and protection, per the authors of *The Color Code*.

Basic Fruit Smoothie

Yields about 1 pint

Combine the following in the blender and blend until smooth:

1 c. nut or seed milk** (or half water, half nut milk)
½ to 1c. fresh or frozen fruit, or a combination***

Optional ingredients:

See list of fortifiers, p. 100.

---

* For this reason older people and people with compromised immunity or weak digestion can benefit from blended foods.

**If nut milk is not available, up to ⅓ cup of presoaked nuts or seeds may be added per cup of pure water.

***See "Proportions for Blood Sugar Balance" on the next page.

Note: If plumped fruit is used, some of the sweet soak water may be included. Use moderately.

Proportions for Blood Sugar Balance

Paying attention to your fruit combinations and proportions will insure the best flavor, texture, digestibility and sugar balance. Refer back to *Fruit Types and Food Combining* on p. 60.

Remember that *sub-acid* fruit combines well with either *acid* fruit or *sweet* fruit. A good ratio of sub-acid fruit to sweet **or** acid fruit is 2:1. With this in mind, I suggest that no more than ¼ cup *sweet* fruit be added to 1 cup of liquid in your smoothie recipe, unless some gel-forming seeds are added to buffer the sugar.

Dried fruit is in the *sweet* category and most remain so even after being plumped. (Some exceptions are elderberries, mulberries, wolfberries and jujube dates, which I would call *sub-acid*.) Plumped fruit is particularly suited for smoothies because it imparts flavor as well as creaminess, to enhance the thinner textures of some of the more common *sub-acid* fruit like apples, pears, cherries and berries. Also, the sweet soak water or syrup made from plumping fruit, stirs in seamlessly, when a little extra sweetening is needed.

Sweet fruit has enough flavor and texture to stand alone, just as long as quantity is limited.

Sweet Fruit Smoothie

Serves 1

1 c. nut or seed milk (or half water, half nut milk)
¼ c. plumped fruit, or ripe sweet fruit (e.g. ½ ripe medium banana)

Blend until you have a texture that you like—a little chunky is good for it encourages chewing. Add any of the optional fortifiers and blend again.

Fortifying Your Smoothies

Smoothies offer not only versatility but the opportunity to palatably incorporate the stronger tasting "good-for-you" foods into your daily diet like the following (suggestions are per 1 to 2 cup serving):

- ¼ tsp. vitamin C crystals
- ¼ to ½ tsp. Siberian Ginseng (*Eleuthero*)—for adults
- 1 tsp. to Tbsp. spirulina (a fresh water, blue-green algae)*
- or other powdered greens**
- 1 tsp. bee pollen
- ⅛ to ¼ tsp. royal jelly
- ½ to 1 tsp. spice or extract
- ¼ tsp. Triphala powder (Ayurvedic—tonic for the colon)
- 1 tsp. dulse flakes or a 2″ piece (source of natural iodine)
- a raw egg from naturally raised, free-ranging hens (see **Note**)
- 1-2 Tbsp. whole chia seeds or ground flaxseeds
- ¼ to ½ c. *Chia Gel* (see next chapter)
- 2 Tbsp. to ¼ c. *Flax Gel* (see next chapter)
- 1 tsp. psyllium husk, whole or powdered
- 1 to 2 Tbsp. flaxseed oil
- 1 tsp. to 1 Tbsp. organic orange or lemon peel
- ¼ to ½ tsp. ground turmeric (anti-inflammatory)
- 1-3 Tbsp. papaya seeds (anti-parasitic)
- 2 tsp. nutritional yeast (*Saccharomyces cerevisiae* strain)
- Replace some or all of the water with *Rejuvelac,* if desired

* Helpful for blood sugar balance, alkalizing chlorophyll, protein, B-complex vitamins and minerals.

**Including chlorella, barley grass, wheat grass, kamut grass, alfalfa. All are alkalizing and offer various other health enhancing properties. Go easy (a teaspoon or less) until you know how much you like.

Note: Raw egg whites contain avidin which blocks the absorption of biotin, an immune protective B-complex vitamin. Eaten in moderation and together with the yolk, which is biotin rich, this should pose no problem. Still some, like myself, may prefer to use only the yolk in its raw form. The separated whites can be saved to use as a binder in cooked foods and baked products. The only truly free-ranging chickens nowadays come from small scale and home flocks, so support your local sources available at green markets, co-ops and from CSA's (to find the ones in your area see sources in **Appendix 2**).

Raw Egg—Care and Benefits

If you tolerate eggs well, you are blessed. Like nuts and seeds, eggs are fortified by Nature to provide the nutrients necessary to create a new life! Eggs are an excellent source of complete protein, in fact, egg protein is the model against which all other proteins are measured. But cooking damages the protein and makes it allergenic to many people. According to Dr. Joseph Mercola, raw eggs are a lot safer than was previously thought, with the chance of salmonella contamination in the eggs of healthy chickens only about 1 in 20,000.

Eggs are also a rich source of pantothenic acid (B_5), biotin, choline, vitamins A, B_1, B_2, B_{12}, D, E, K, iron, manganese, zinc and the detoxifying sulfur-containing amino acids. Use only organic eggs from free-ranging chickens for they are healthier, thanks to their ability to forage. Eggs from chickens that have been fed flaxseeds are higher in the Omega-3 fatty acids.

Discard eggs that are cracked, have watery yolks or an off odor. Wash shells before cracking, if dirty. If you would like added safety assurance, add a few drops of stabilized oxygen (O_7) or sodium chlorite, per egg yolk to kill bacteria (not more than 10 drops/cup of liquid). Blend yolk, drops and nut milk together before adding fruit or the antioxidants in the fruit will deactivate the O_7. Consume promptly or refrigerate.

Getting More from Organically Grown Citrus

Chop orange and lemon peels and freeze in small bags. They can also be air dried but frozen taste better, retain more nutrients and are easier to use.

Add frozen to foods that will be cooked or run water over them to thaw quickly. For a finer texture, grind the frozen peels in the blender or food processor. Use to add zest to fruit salads, smoothies and s/cereals, or in cookies, cakes, waffles, etc. They contain vitamin C and bioflavonoids (vitamin P), important for strong connective tissues and capillaries. Bioflavonoids are also anti-inflammatory and enhance vitamin C activity.

F.Y.I. The peels also contain essential oils, which are alkaline-forming and immune supportive. Some constituents like limonene are potent cancer fighters, per *The Color Code*.

Fruit Smoothies

Blueberry/Pineapple Smoothie

Blueberries (ORAC 2,400) are rich in phytonutrients. One test showed that feeding subjects blueberries helped to reverse brain aging and several studies have shown improvement in learning and physical abilities—thus their nickname, "brain berries."

Blueberry/Pineapple Smoothie

Serves 1

Combine in the blender and process to the texture that you like:

½ to 1 c. fresh or frozen blueberries
½ c. pineapple, fresh chunks
1 c. nut or seed milk

Enjoy for a quick, nutritious breakfast or a refreshing snack.

Variations: Replace blueberries with cherries. Sweeten to taste with a little maple, or low glycemic agave, syrup.

This is a thick smoothie. Its deep rich color bears witness to its phyto-power. The addition of bananas, whether fresh or frozen, imparts a sweet creaminess to smoothies. The bananas may be replaced by plumped fruit (see next page).

Verry Berry Smoothie

Yields 3 to 4 cups

1 c. water
1 c. nut milk
1 banana
2 c. fresh or frozen berries

Combine the banana with water and milk and blend. Then add berries, 1 cup at a time, and blend again each time to incorporate.

Blueberry *Verry Berry Smoothie*

According to Dr. Peter D'Adamo (author of Eat Right 4 Your Type*), people with blood type A should avoid bananas. Plumped fruit, or a smooth textured fruit like ripe peach or mango, can be substituted for ripe banana in any of these recipes.*

Sesame/Carob Smoothie

Yields 1½ cups

1 Tbsp. tahini (any type)
1 c. water
¼ c. *sweet* fruit (½ ripe banana, or ¼ c. plumped fruit)
1 Tbsp. roasted carob powder, or 1 Tbsp. *Carob Syrup* (see p. 90)

Combine in the blender and process for about 1 minute.

Carob/Banana Smoothie

Yields 1 pint

Combine in the blender and process to the texture that you like:
1 c. nut milk
½ ripe banana
1 to 2 Tbsp. carob powder, or 1 Tbsp. *Carob Syrup* (p. 90)
1 tsp. vanilla extract (optional)

If you would like to thicken further stir in 1 to 2 Tbsp. *Chia Gel.*

Flaxseed Shake (Flaxative)

Serves 1

Combine in a jar or in the blender:
¼ c. whole flaxseeds
½ c. water

Let stand for 2-8 hours (or overnight), then add:
½ c. more water (hot or cold)
½ to 1 ripe banana or ¼ to ⅓ c. plumped fruit

Blend with a stop-start action until thick and creamy. Enjoy. Refrigerate leftovers for a pudding-like snack.

Fig or Prune Whip

Serves 1

Combine in the blender and process to the texture that you like:

1 c. nut milk, or half water and half nut milk
¼ c. plumped figs* or pitted prunes

Then you can add a raw egg yolk, flax or chia seed, or whatever is desired.

Figgy/Berry Smoothie

Yields about 3 cups

Combine in the blender and blend:

1 c. water
½ c. plumped figs*

Then add the following and blend again:

1 c. nut milk
½ c. fresh or frozen berries

Optional additions:
1 to 2 raw egg yolks—add last.

Strawberry/Pear Smoothie (see photo on p. 97)

Yields approximately 3 cups

Combine in the blender and process to the texture that you like:

1 c. nut milk
1 pear, quartered, with blossom end removed
½ c. strawberries, fresh or frozen

Variation: Replace pear with 1 peach or nectarine (pitted), include skin only if organically grown.

---

* Calmyrna figs are sweeter than Black Mission figs, which contain more iron. Either can be used.

Mango Momma Smoothie made with nut milk and frozen raspberries.

Mangoes are the most popular fruit in the world! They are sweet but low in calories, contain a wealth of vitamin C and are a low-fat source of vitamin E.* If this were not enough, their flavor and texture are exquisite! In fact, I find them so irresistible that mine hardly ever last long enough to make this.

Mango Momma Smoothie

Yields about 1 pint

1 c. water or nut milk
½ ripe mango, cubed
½ c. strawberries, raspberries or cherries
2 Tbsp. ground flaxseeds, or 1 Tbsp. ground chia seeds (optional)

Combine all ingredients and blend to the desired consistency.

* From *Wellness Foods A to Z*, a UC Berkeley *Wellness Letter Book*.

For Love of Mangoes

Momma never fed me mangoes.

Perhaps she knew

that mangoes

are a fruit of passion.

I like mine tinted

green and red

yielding to gentle pressure

with a sweet earthy scent.

I peel, then cut,

smooth, creamy slices.

The juice is just sweet enough.

The flesh that's close to the pit is fibrous.

I hold it over a bowl

and pull it between my teeth

as orange, sweet juice runs

down my chin and hands--

mmm-mmm good!

I lick my fingers

one at a time

then I lick my bowl,

giving Thanks,

tasting, praising.

Such is my love

of mangoes!

Ripe mango is so delectable! Slice along the pit, score, then reflex the skin
to eat out of hand, or cut for fruit salads or smoothies.

*The next two smoothies are minimally sweet but pleasantly flavorful and
high in antioxidants. Papaya seeds are peppery and anti-parasitic. Eaten
in such small proportion with the flesh, their flavor adds only a subtle nuance.*

Papaya Smoothie

Yields about 2½ cups

Combine in the blender and process for 2 minutes
½ c. almond milk
1 c. ripe papaya chunks
1 to 2 tablespoons papaya seeds
½ c. water
1 Tbsp. flaxseed, ground

This recipe is very filling and might be sufficient to serve 2.

Wolfberries (goji berries) are high in protein and antioxidants and only mildly sweet. Regular consumption can improve eyesight. I recommend plumping them before using in fruit salads, smoothies and s/cereals to soften their tiny seeds and make them easier to chew. (See **Chapter 3** *for more information.)*

Wolfberry Smoothie

Serves 1

1 c. nut or seed milk
½ c. plumped wolfberries, including some of the syrup (soak water)
½ banana, or sweetener of choice (optional)

Combine in the blender and process to the texture that you like. Add a fortifier, if desired. I like to add an egg yolk.

Wolfberry Smoothie--unsweetened, with egg yolk.

Fruit and Vegetable Smoothies

Delicious and alkalizing smoothies may also be made from blended vegetables with a little fruit added to balance the flavor. These might be preferable to persons who have problems with fruit sugars. Though technically raw fruit and vegetables do not combine well, when blended they seem quite digestible. The veggies help to bring the sugar content down and the nutrient content up. Below is my version of Dr. Ann Wigmore's famous *Energy Soup*, a blended salad.

Over a decade ago, when I was sick with a digestive problem I found that this was one of the few foods that I could digest easily, without discomfort. In fact, it felt as though my cells welcomed it and literally "sucked it up!" Leaving it a little chunky encourages chewing and stimulates a greater secretion of enzymes in the mouth.

Energy Soup

Yields about 1 pint

Combine in the blender:
1 apple or other fruit in season, approximately ½ to 1 c. (peeled if inorganic)
2 c. water*
2 c. wild and/or organic greens**, washed thoroughly under running
 water
½ avocado, or ½ c. presoaked seeds or nuts

Blend first two ingredients on low, using "stop/start" action to get it going, then increase power. Add remaining ingredients and blend until you have the consistency you like. Eat immediately for the greatest benefit.

---

* Dr. Ann always used a fermented grain beverage, in this recipe, but the quality of mine varied so much that I finally stopped using it and replaced it with water. If you would like to try your hand at it, see directions for *Rejuvelac* on p. 35.

**Always remove any tough, fibrous parts because, unlike Green Drink, this does not get strained. See recommended greens in the box on the next page.

Choosing Your Greens

Choose tender leaves from: parsley, cilantro*, endive, escarole, romaine lettuce, dandelion, wild lettuce, chickory, spinach, chard, purslane, mallow, field daisy, chickweed, plantain, sorrel (small amount), amaranth, lambsquarters, yellow or sour dock, violet, sow thistle.

Avoid cruciferous (cabbage family) greens if you have or suspect that you have an underactive (hypo-) thyroid, for they contain a natural chemical—goitrogen—which blocks iodine absorption in the thyroid. Especially high are: cabbage, Brussels sprouts, cauliflower, mustard greens and turnip tops.

* Known to chelate lead, mercury and aluminum and take it out of the body through the urine.

Though avocado is technically a fruit, I included it in this section because it is high in protein and fat and low in sugar, unlike other fruit. Avocados contain inulin, an indigestible carbohydrate that does not raise blood sugar levels.

This has a lovely pastel green color and a fresh mild flavor. It is a little thicker than the nut or seed milks and lower in protein.

Avocado Milk/Smoothie

Yields 1 quart

1 c. water
½ *Haas* avocado (a California variety)
1 tsp. lemon juice (to prevent discoloration from oxidation)
about 3 c. additional water

Blend first three ingredients together until creamy, then add more water to make a quart. Use in place of nut or seed milk on fruit salads or cereals, or as a beverage. Store in the refrigerator and shake before serving.

Avocado Milk/Smoothie

Avocados are high in monounsaturated fatty acids, the kind that lower LDL cholesterol. They are also power houses of other nutrients like B vitamins, especially folate, and potassium and have more protein than other fruit. Ounce per ounce, Florida avocados have about half the fat and ⅔ the calories of California varieties, per *The Wellness Encyclopedia of Food and Nutrition*.

Avocado/Pineapple Smoothie

Serves 1

1 c. avocado milk, or 1 c. water and ⅛ avocado
1 c. pineapple*, cubed

Add ¼ tsp. lemon juice if water and a piece of avocado are used instead of the milk. Blend until smooth.

* Fresh pineapples are high in fruit acids which can etch the teeth so it is helpful to get into the habit of rinsing the mouth with water after consuming them.

Chapter 6
The Gel-forming Seeds

3 Seed Sereal made with Brazil nut milk.

The Gel-forming Seeds

Gel-forming fiber is the soluble, *mucilaginous* fiber in some seeds, grains, vegetables and fruits that traps water and creates a clear slippery gel which lubricates the digestive tract, bowel and the joints. This fiber is thirsty for water so it needs to be well hydrated before consuming, or it will become drying and irritating to the G.I. tract.

Soluble fiber is, notably, helpful in the treatment of cardiovascular disease, obesity and diabetes. It is cholesterol lowering. It is filling and creates a physical barrier between carbohydrates and the digestive enzymes that break them down, slowing the conversion of carbs to sugar*. This mucilage also does something very helpful for persons with food allergies and sensitivities. It mechanically buffers the digestive tract from the effects of toxic or irritating food ingredients. It also soothes inflamed tissue.

These recipes feature the following: chia seeds, flaxseeds and psyllium (pronounced *silly-um*) seed husks. While these recipes combine the seeds with liquid for use in fruit meals, you may receive their many benefits** by just combining them with liquid and drinking before one or more meals daily.

Simple Seed Drinks

Serves 1

To 1 c. water (or 50/50 water and juice) add one of the following:

1 t. psyllium seed husk powder (or a rounded tsp. if whole husks)
1 to 1½ tsp. chia seed (whole)
1 to 1½ Tbsp. flaxseed, ground

Stir or shake to combine seeds and water. Drink immediately if psyllium seed drink. Let stand for 10 to 15 minutes if ground flaxseed, and 15 minutes or longer if chia.

Cautions: Do not take supplements or medications with these drinks. Some may prefer to take their fiber in capsules. If so, please be sure to take with 1 or 2 cups of water and drink plenty of water throughout the day.

* Also helpful for endurance athletes for the same reason.

**These seeds also provide insoluble fiber which helps with regularity and normalizes stool consistency.

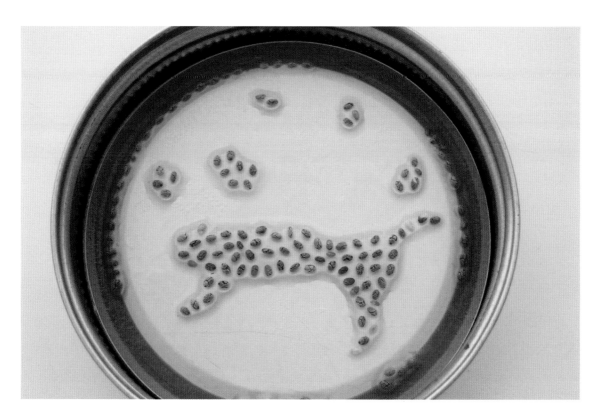

A clear gel is formed when chia seeds are mixed with water.

Chia Seeds

Chia seeds* (photo above) were recognized by the Aztecs, Mayans and Native Americans of the Southwestern United States as a super food, one that could sustain a warrior or runner for many days or restore health to the sick or dying. They are high in both insoluble and soluble, gel-forming fiber, complete protein, calcium**, iron and B-complex vitamins. Though high in fat, it is over 60% Omega-3 unsaturated fatty acid (alpha-linolenic), making chia seed oil the richest in this anti-inflammatory, immune supportive and heart protective fat.

Unlike flaxseeds and psyllium seeds, which need to be ground to make their nutrients available or palatable, chia seeds need only to be combined with liquid. When prepared in this way chia seeds are more than 90% water and have a tapioca-like texture. Add to cereals, fruits, smoothies, nut butters, mayonnaise, salad dressings, puddings and desserts for the beneficial fiber and to reduce calories, or just stir into water or juice for a healthful beverage.

*Yes, they are the same seeds that are commonly used to grow "Chia Pets"!

**By weight, they contain five times the calcium of milk.

Native Americans of the Desert Southwest may be our modern equivalent to the canaries in the coal mines. They experienced a rise in diabetes and associated problems after adopting the white man's low fiber diet chocked with sugar, white flour products and other refined foods. It has only been through the return to their native, high fiber, unrefined diet that they have seen real progress in reversing this disease. Wild chia seeds were a traditional staple.

Today, chia seeds are cultivated in South and Central America without the use of chemicals, pesticides, or herbicides. I have seen them in some natural supermarkets. If not available in your area you can order them (see **Appendix 2** for suppliers).

For a romantic and informative account of this little known miracle food and recipes, see *The Magic of Chia--Revival of an Ancient Wonder Food*, by James F. Scheer (2001). The following two recipes are taken from this book. They are both easy ways to begin to experience the many benefits of this remarkable food. (All of the recipes from Scheer's book and more information about benefits for athletes—including hydration and electrolyte balance—are available from the website http://menu4life.anthill.com/.)

Chia Water

Serves 1

1 tsp. to 1 Tbsp. chia seeds
1 c. water

Stir seed into water and let stand overnight. Drink as is, or combine with juice, in the morning.

Note: Always add the seed to the water, rather than the water to the seed, to prevent seeds from sticking together.

Grinding Chia Seeds

Chia seeds can be ground in the blender a cup at a time, or in a seed mill in smaller quantities. Make sure that the blending container is dry. They have more antioxidants than flaxseeds so are more stable once ground. Store in a tightly closed container in the refrigerator. Ground seeds will absorb water faster than whole seeds. The nutrients in ground seeds are also more readily available than those in whole seeds.

The following is so beneficial and versatile that you might want to keep some on hand to combine with other more calorie dense foods. The gel gives body and a pleasant texture while buffering fruit sugars. It keeps in the refrigerator for up to 2 weeks.

Chia Gel

Yields 3 cups

¼ c. chia seeds
2½ c. water

In a bowl or quart jar, sprinkle the seeds over cold water and whisk or shake to moisten. Let stand for 5 minutes then whisk or shake again. Let stand for at least 15 minutes to set up, or cover and let stand overnight. Store in the refrigerator.

Chia gel may be added to juices, fruit salads, smoothies, s/cereals, jams, jellies and fruit purees to thicken and add smoothness, to buffer sugars and to fortify.

Chia Fresca is a refreshing Mexican drink made with lime juice, or lime water, and chia seeds. This version is thicker and turns a little juice into a filling snack.

Chia Fresca

Serves 1

Stir 1 to 2 Tbsp. of freshly squeezed lemon or lime juice into about ½ cup *Chia Gel*, then stir in enough water to make 1 cup.

Note: *Chia Gel* is tasteless and has a remarkable quality of taking on added flavors without diluting them. A small amount of fruit juice is enough to flavor ½ cup of gel.

The tapioca-like texture of the gel is damaged by blending so stir it into food after blending if you want to keep this consistency.

Flaxseeds

Flaxseeds are also a super food. There are at least two varieties, chocolate brown and golden. According the Canadian Flax Council, there is little difference in food value. Like chia seeds, they contain all of the eight essential amino acids and are a rich vegetal source of Omega-3's. Flaxseeds also contain lignans, phyto-compounds which help to balance hormones, protect against cancer, free-radical damage and atherosclerosis.

The oil is anti-inflammatory and helps to normalize cholesterol. It is also quite fragile, easily becoming rancid, so always keep it refrigerated. Buy "fresh pressed, organic oil" and use it up quickly (within four months of the pressing date). The "use by" date should be on the bottle as should the pressing date. Additionally, do not use direct heat on flaxseed oil--do not fry or sauté with it. Add it to salads, shakes, dressings, or use it instead of butter on cooked grains, beans, veggies, popcorn or breads. Add just before serving to soups and stews for added body and staying power.

I prefer to use the whole seed for it has a protective hull that allows for safe storage at room temperature, until cracked. In addition, it contains beneficial fiber, nutrients and protein not available in the oil. It is also a fraction of the cost of the oil. Approximately 5 tablespoons of seeds provide 1 tablespoon of oil.

Presoaking the whole seeds in water for 2 or more hours, or grinding a small quantity at a time are the easiest ways to start to include flaxseeds in your daily food. The presoaked seeds make delicious, creamy smoothies and puddings (no need for dairy or eggs), while the ground seeds can be stirred into cereals or soups, or added to juices or smoothies. Any surplus ground seeds should be stored in the freezer in a tightly sealed, vapor-proof bag or container.

Note: Water/liquid is an important addition to flaxseed-containing foods and beverages because of the seed's rich and unique fiber content. Avoid cold cereals that contain whole flaxseeds unless you plan to let them soak for at least 10 minutes before eating, for they can be irritating to the digestive tract.

Do not buy ground flaxseed, or foods that contain them, unless they are nitrogen sealed. Be sure to keep them refrigerated or frozen once opened.

Flax Gel

Yields 1 cup

Soak ¼ cup whole flaxseed in ½ cup water for 2 to 8 hours. Place in blender with ½ cup more water and blend until smooth. Store in the refrigerator. This keeps 2-3 days.

Stir flax gel into fruit salads or cooked cereals, dressings or sauces that will be eaten quickly, or blend into smoothies.

Flaxseed Egg Replacer--Use ¼ cup (4 Tbsp.) *Flax Gel* to replace 1 medium egg in baked products.

Grinding Dry Flaxseed

Flaxseeds go rancid quickly, so fresh daily grinding of small quantities is best. A coffee or seed grinder works well for this purpose.

If you will be using larger quantities or do not have one of the above-mentioned grinders, a blender works well, also, for grinding flaxseed into a fine meal. You will want to store it in the freezer in a tightly sealed plastic bag (zip locks are perfect) or other container with a tight seal e.g. a glass jar with a rubber gasket in the lid, to minimize the oxidating effects of air.

Make sure your blender is perfectly dry. For optimal grinding action you will need about a cup of seeds. Blend on high speed for about 30 seconds. Stop the blender and stir with a chopstick or butter knife, then cover and grind for another 30 seconds.

Psyllium Seed Husks

Psyllium contains both soluble and insoluble fiber thus it is beneficial for regularity as well as cardiovascular health. It absorbs many times its volume in water, thus one should combine it with water or drink plenty of water to keep it from drying the system out.

Psyllium is perhaps best known as an ingredient in *Metamucil*™, where it acts as a mechanical laxative i.e. a bulking agent. It actually is quite balancing for the stools, softening hard stools and giving form to loose stools. Its high content of soluble, gel-forming fiber makes it soothing to the G.I. tract and cholesterol lowering.

Whole psyllium seeds may be purchased for sprouting, but they are not very palatable. As a food, the husk is more acceptable and it is used mostly as a filler or binder. It is itself tasteless, so does not interfere with the flavors of other ingredients, unless to mute them slightly. It works nicely in *seed sereals*, smoothies and as a binder in wheat-free baked products.

Psyllium seed husks are available whole or powdered. The powdered husks will absorb more water than an equal volume of whole husks.

Notes of Caution

Whenever a new food is being added to the diet, one needs to proceed slowly and to pay attention. I recommend that you begin experimenting with the gel-forming seeds, one at a time to see how you react to each.

Always be sure to combine them with water before consuming or they will draw moisture from your digestive tract and can cause irritation or possibly blockage in some people.

Do not take supplements or medications with psyllium, flax or chia seed drinks for their action is to move things through and out of the digestive tract.

Always consume plenty of water throughout the day.

Grated apple with black mission figs, wolfberries and nut milk

Goji Berry Breakfast

Serves 1

Combine all in a cereal bowl:
½ to 1 apple or pear (sliced or grated), including seeds
2 Tbsp. wolfberries (goji berries), plumped*
4 black mission figs, plumped, sliced (optional)
1 to 2 Tbsp. chia or ground flaxseeds
¾ to 1 c. nut or seed milk

Let stand for 5 to 10 minutes to allow the seeds to absorb moisture and thicken the mixture before eating.

Optional: 1 tsp. to 1 Tbsp. organic orange or lemon peel and/or 1 tsp. bee pollen. A small handful presoaked nuts or 1 tablespoon seeds. Substitute currants, raisins or other berries for wolfberries.

* See info about wolfberries and plumping dried fruits in **Chapter 3.**

Seed Sereals

I call these *sereals* because they are made from seeds rather than from cereal grains. They are low in starch so instead of raising your blood sugar and cholesterol, they will assist in the creation and maintenance of balance in both. They are a simple and versatile answer to the need to provide healthful, high fiber, nutrient dense alternatives to grains and overly processed cereals.

Simple Seed Sereals

Serves 1

To ½ cup of water or nut milk add **one** of the following:
1 to 1½ Tbsp. chia seeds, or
3 to 4 Tbsp. ground flaxseeds, or
1 tsp. psyllium husk (whole)

Stir seeds into liquid in a serving bowl. Let stand for 5 to 15 minutes. The gel thickness will be similar to applesauce. Layer fruit/berries on top. Serve with presoaked nuts or seeds, or nut milk.

Clockwise from upper left:
Chia seed, ground golden flaxseed and psyllium seed husk flakes

The recipes below are very filling because of the expansive fiber, high protein and good fat content found in the seeds.

Flaxy Lady Sereal

Serves 1 to 2

In a cereal bowl, stir together the following:
¼ c. ground flaxseeds
1 rounded tsp. psyllium husks (whole)
1 tsp. to 1 Tbsp. date sugar (optional)

Then quickly whisk in 1 cup pure water (warm the water in cold weather). Allow to stand for 3 to 5 minutes to thicken and develop the beneficial gel. Serve with sliced fresh fruit or a combination of fresh and plumped fruit and nut milk.

The following is warm and satisfying though not really cooked.

Hearty Flaxseed Sereal

Serves 1 to 2

1 c. boiling water
⅓ c. ground flaxseeds
½ to 1 tsp. kelp or dulse, granules or flakes (optional)
2 Tbsp. dried fruit pieces, or 1 Tbsp. date sugar (optional)

Remove water from heat source. Whisk the dry ingredients into the boiling water, cover and let stand for 5 minutes. Serve with nut or seed milk.

Carob/Flaxseed Pudding

Yields about 1 pint

¼ c. flaxseeds, whole
1½ c. water
2 to 4 Tbsp. carob powder
1 ripe banana
½ to 1 tsp. dulse, granules or flakes (optional)

Combine the seeds and water and let stand for 2 hours or more. Then blend with the remaining ingredients until creamy.

Hot *2 Seed Sereal* with chia, flax and dulse--*Sucanat*™ on top.

This makes a quick and satisfying hot sereal, though it can also be made with room temperature water.

2 Seed Sereal

Serves 1 to 2

1 c. water
a combination of any two: 2 Tbsp. each ground flax or ground chia seeds
    or 1 to 2 tsp. psyllium husk
1 to 2 Tbsp. black currants, or raisins, etc.

Bring water to a boil. In a bowl combine seeds and fruit. Remove water from heat source and whisk in seed mixture, cover and let stand for 5 minutes. Serve with nut milk and fresh fruit, or a sweetener, if desired.

Optional additions to seed mixture: ½ to 1 tsp. dulse flakes, or a pinch of salt, 1 Tbsp. date sugar, dash of spice.

3 Seed Sereal made with golden flaxseed

The following has the consistency of tapioca pudding. While it can be prepared as a quick breakfast, it tastes best and is most beneficial if it is prepared the night before.

3 Seed Sereal

Yields about 1¾ cups (2 to 4 servings)

1 tsp. to 1 Tbsp. psyllium, whole husk (1 Tbsp. used in photo)
2 Tbsp. chia seeds
3 Tbsp. ground flaxseeds
1 Tbsp. date sugar (optional)
1½ c. water or nut milk

Stir dry ingredients together in a bowl, then stir in water. Let stand for 10 to 15 minutes, or overnight, covered. Stir again, briskly with a fork or whisk before serving. Serve plain or with fruit and nut milk.

Strawberry/Nectarine Breakfast

I love the silky smooth skin and the sweet juicy flesh of nectarines, close cousins of peaches. While low in calories, they are high in potassium, fiber and the antioxidants beta carotene and beta cryptoxanthin. They pair up nicely with berries of all kinds. Crack the "stone" open with a hammer or rubber mallet to remove the edible kernel.

Strawberry/Nectarine Breakfast

Serves 1

½ to 1 c. *3 Seed Sereal (recipe on previous page made with 1 tsp. psyllium, whole husk)*
1 nectarine, sliced
handful of strawberries, sliced

Combine ingredients in a bowl. Serve as is or top with a handful of presoaked nuts or seeds, or nut milk.

Mango/Blackberry Breakfast with *Almond Milk*

Mango/Blackberry Breakfast

Serves 1

½ ripe mango, peeled and cubed
1 handful blackberries, fresh
½ c. *3 Seed Sereal*

Place sereal in a bowl and add fruit. Serve with nut milk and presoaked almonds, if desired.

Berries are power houses for nutrients and anti-oxidants. Fresh is best and frozen is next. Take care to prevent mold growth. Store fresh berries dry, in ventilated containers for a day or two. Wash just before serving. Freeze and/or process into jam if you have a large quantity.

Lightly Cooked Breakfast Puddings

Many find that they prefer a warm breakfast or that fruits digest better for them if lightly cooked. During cold and/or damp times I prefer this method also. The fiber *sereal* and nut milk will not be cooked, so you will still be getting their enzymes and cleansing power. I call these thickened compotes "breakfast puddings." There are also non-fruit versions for those who want/need to avoid fruit (see "**Veggie Variation**" in the box below).

Basic Breakfast Pudding

¼ to ½ c. water
1 to 3 c. raw sliced or grated fruit (may include plumped fruit and berries)
½ to 1 c. any presoaked fiber s/cereal e.g. *Chia Gel, Flaxseed Sereal, 3 Seed Sereal* (recipes in this chapter) or *Precious Gump* (p. 139).

Heat water to boil. Add fruit, cover pot and simmer for 2 or 3 minutes—just enough to soften slightly and warm. Stir in fiber cereal, cover and turn off the heat. Let stand a few minutes to warm the fiber s/cereal. Serve plain or with nut milk (see previous chapter).

Veggie Variation: Start with at least ½ c. water and substitute grated veggies for all or part of the fruit and cook for 5 minutes or longer to soften. Grate root veggies finely for faster cooking. If combining with fruit or a faster cooking veggie, like zucchini or summer squash, give the root a 3 to 5 minute head start, or just use leftover cooked veggies. See *Apple/Zucchini, Sweet Potato, Happy Beets* and *Squash Breakfast Pudding* recipes below.

Note: I recommend that these be cooked in non-metal cookware for fruit acids react to metal, leaching them into the food—especially avoid aluminum, copper, cast iron and pitted or scratched *Teflon*™ or stainless steel cookware for fruits. My personal preference is enameled cast iron, e.g. *Le Creuset*™.

Plum/Apple Breakfast Pudding

Yields about 3 cups

½ c. water
1 cinnamon stick, 3" (optional)
2 to 3 plums, sliced
1 apple, grated
1 c. *3 Seed Sereal*

Add cinnamon stick to water and bring to a boil in a 1 quart non-metal saucepan. Add fruit, cover and simmer for 1 to 2 minutes. Stir in *Sereal*, cover and turn off the heat. Let stand for a few minutes. Serve as is or with nut milk.

See **"Veggie Variation"** on p. 128.

Plum/Apple Breakfast Pudding

Crunchy Apple/Goji Pudding

Yields about 2 cups

⅓ c. water
1 cinnamon stick, 3" (optional)
1 apple, grated
⅓ c. plumped goji berries (wolfberries) or raisins, etc.
1 Tbsp. decorticated apricot kernels, or sunflower or pumpkin seeds
1 c. *Precious Gump* (see p. 139)

Bring water to a boil with cinnamon stick, if desired, in a 1 quart non-metal saucepan. Add fruit, cover and simmer for 1 to 2 minutes. Stir in *Gump*, cover and turn off the heat. Let stand for a few minutes. Serve as is or with nut milk.

Variation: For a thicker pudding, stir in 1 Tbsp. chia or ground flaxseeds at the same time as *Gump*. To sweeten top with 1 tsp. *Sucanat*™ (dehydrated organic sugar cane) or honey.

Crunchy Apple/Goji Pudding with *Sucanat*™ and *Almond Milk*

Pear and Red (Jujube) Date Pudding
Serves 1

¼ c. water
1 pear, diced
1 small handful red (jujube)* dates
½ c. *Precious Gump* (see p. 139)

Bring water to a boil in a 1 quart non-metal saucepan. Add fruit, cover and simmer for 2 to 3 minutes. Stir in *Gump*, cover and turn off the heat. Let stand for a few minutes. Serve as is or with a dash of spice and/or nut milk.

Pear and Red (Jujube) Date Pudding

* Jujube dates are considered a tonic food in Traditional Chinese Medicine, which focuses on the healing qualities of foods. They are less sweet than brown dates and are said to be purifying to the twelve organ meridians, to improve circulation and tone up the stomach, heart and lungs. Available from *Crimson Dragon Herbs* (see **Appendix 2**).

Apple/Zucchini Breakfast Pudding

Yields about 3 cups

½ c. water
1 cinnamon stick, 3" (optional)
1 c. grated zucchini
1 small or medium apple, grated (about 2 c.)
1 c. *Precious Gump* **or** *3 Seed Sereal*

Add cinnamon stick to water and bring to a boil in a 1 quart non-metal saucepan. Add zucchini first, cover and simmer for 3 to 5 minutes. Add apple, cover and cook for a minute or two more. Remove from heat and immediately and stir in *Gump* or *Sereal*; let stand for a few minutes to warm the fiber s/cereal. Serve as is or with nut milk.

Sweet Potato Breakfast Pudding

Yields 2+ cups

½ c. water
2 to 3 c. sweet potato, grated
1 c. *3 Seed Sereal*
a dash of salt, or 1 tsp. dulse flakes (optional)

Bring water to a boil in a 1 quart non-metal saucepan. Add sweet potato, cover and simmer for about 5 to 8 minutes or until tender (the more finely grated, the faster it will cook). Remove from heat and immediately stir in *sereal* and salt, or dulse. Let stand for a few minutes. Serve with flaxseed oil, a little cold-pressed oil, or a pat of butter or ghee, and a dash of your favorite spice.

Variation: Replace all or part of the sweet potato with grated winter squash, or a sweet root veggie like carrot, beet or parsnip, or a combination.

Happy Beets Breakfast Pudding

Serves 1

½ c. water
1½ c. grated beet
1 Tbsp. chopped organic orange peel
1½ c. grated apple
2 Tbsp. plumped wolfberries, raisins or currants
½ c. *Chia Gel*
a dash of salt (optional)

Bring water to a boil, add beets and cover. Simmer for about 5 minutes then add orange peel and cook for a few minutes more. Add apples and berries, and cook for 1 to 2 minutes. Turn off the heat, stir in gel, cover and let stand for a minute or two, if desired. Stir in salt and serve. Garnish with fresh orange rind. (I like mine served with 1 to 2 tsp. flax seed oil, 1 tsp. honey and a dash of spice.)

This is made a little differently than the above, but I wanted to include it here because winter squash is such an overlooked breakfast natural! This is best if the squash is taken hot from the oven. I like to include pieces of tender squash rind, also.

Squash Breakfast Pudding
Serves 1

½ to 1 c. baked buttercup squash
½ to ¾ c. *Precious Gump* (p. 139)
2 tsp. to 1 Tbsp. flaxseed oil
dash of spice of choice (optional)
2 tsp. maple syrup, or sweetener of choice (optional)
1 Tbsp. lightly toasted coconut (optional)

Combine *Precious Gump* and squash in a cereal bowl. Add oil and spice, then top with a little sweetener, and/or lightly toasted coconut, if desired.

Variations: Substitute your favorite winter squash. If using leftover squash, begin by heating it with a little water or broth.

Chapter 7
Uncooked Cereals

Precious Gump made with oat bran and chia seeds

Uncooked Cereals

Cereals, technically grains of the grass family, have been way overdone as breakfast foods and we are seeing more and more about how they raise blood sugar and cause various other problems from celiac disease to arthritis (see *Going Against the Grain*, by Melissa Diane Smith and *The No-Grain Diet*, by Dr. Joseph Mercola).

If you tolerate grains well, they can be presoaked overnight in twice as much water, with ½ teaspoon citric acid per pint of water to kill mold. In the morning drain and rinse, then you can proceed to sprout, blend or just eat as is. For some, uncooked grains will digest too fast and raise blood sugar, unless combined with some nuts, seeds or another form of protein and/or fat. Cooking whole grains slows their digestion, also.

New Bran Cereals

I do think that in our age of digestive and degenerative problems, such as diabetes, obesity and heart disease, the nutrient and fiber rich bran found in grains might provide more value than the starchy endosperm.

As always, if you are not accustomed to eating these foods, some caution is advisable to give your digestive tract an opportunity to adjust. Some may notice more flatulence or bloating when beginning a high fiber diet. While the presoaking process will facilitate the digestion and utilization of these new foods, some may benefit from taking a digestive enzyme containing cellulase in the beginning.

Phytate: The outer coating of all seeds contain phytates which bind with minerals preventing absorption. When bran is presoaked in water overnight the phytic acid is deactivated.

Storage Tip: Store bran in the refrigerator or freezer to prevent rancidity and insect infestation.

Note: Room temperature water is used in these recipes unless otherwise indicated.

A Comparison of Brans

Oat bran contains *gluten** and both insoluble and soluble** (cholesterol lowering), mucilaginous fiber. It also contains silica, protein and fat.

Rice bran is *gluten-free*, contains heart friendly fats, including gamma oryzanol, from the germ. In addition, it is a rich source of iron, B-vitamins and contains soluble and insoluble fiber.

Wheat bran contains *gluten*, magnesium, potassium, iron, selenium and some protein. It is the highest in insoluble (stool bulking) fiber, which can be harsh if not combined with a soothing, mucilaginous fiber like psyllium, chia or ground flaxseeds. Some persons sensitive to the endosperm of wheat seem to be able to use the bran especially when presoaked and combined as in the *Precious Gump*, p. 139.

To Kill Bacteria and Mold

Some persons with compromised immune systems and/or mold sensitivity may prefer to add the following to the bran cereals in this section.

For bacteria--8 to 10 drops stabilized oxygen (O_7) drops, per pint
For mold--½ tsp. citric acid, per pint

Note: Do not add oxygen drops to hot foods, heat deactivates. If both citric acid and O_7 are to be used, first add the O_7, wait a minute or two, then stir in the citric acid, for antioxidants also deactivate O_7.

---

* Oats, in their pure form, are gluten-free but become contaminated during commercial processing.

**Soluble fiber has a smooth consistency when combined with water, while insoluble fiber will still have rough edges.

The following soaked fiber cereal is surprisingly nutritious--⅓ c. oat bran has 95 calories, 2.5g total fat (.5g saturated), 7g protein and 6g fiber (both soluble and insoluble). While it may be ready after only 5 minutes of soaking, the longer soaking time suggested breaks down the phytates found in all brans. Though oat bran contains gluten, many persons sensitive to wheat gluten tolerate oat bran, perhaps because of the protective function of its mucilaginous soluble fiber.

Simple Oat Bran Cereal *(contains gluten)*

Serves 1

Combine in a bowl or jar, cover and let stand overnight (refrigerate during hot weather):
⅓ c. oat bran
1 c. water

Serve as is, or add fresh fruit and nut milk; for some palates no milk is needed, for when mixed with water, oat bran produces a milky liquid.

Variations: To increase the soluble fiber, use only ¼ c. bran and add 1 Tbsp. chia seeds, or 1½ to 2 Tbsp. ground flaxseeds. For extra iodine, iron, protein and a little bit of salt, stir in ½ to 1 tsp. dulse flakes. Instead of fresh fruit: add 1 tsp. to 1 Tbsp. date sugar, or 1 Tbsp. raisins or dried berries, date pieces or chopped dried fruit and soak overnight, or stir in plumped fruit before serving.

Simple Rice Bran Cereal *(gluten-free)*

Serves 1

Combine in a bowl or jar, cover and let stand overnight (refrigerate during hot weather):
⅓ c. rice bran
1 c. water

Serve as is, or add fresh fruit and nut milk.

See **Variations** above.

The following will help to balance the bowels and maintain regularity. Animals have benefited from it too. Cats seem to like it with kelp added.

Precious Gump *(see photo at beginning of chapter)*

Combine in a pint jar:

½ c. oat bran **or** rice bran; **or** ¾ c. raw wheat bran*
1 Tbsp. psyllium husk powder (or 1 rounded Tbsp. whole psyllium husks)
   or 2 Tbsp. chia seeds **or** 4 Tbsp. ground flaxseeds

Fill jar to top with pure water, stir and add more water to top. Let stand, covered, at room temperature (or refrigerate)** overnight.

Serve about ½ to 1 cup for breakfast with sliced fresh fruit, berries or plumped (reconstituted) fruit and nut or seed milk. Store remainder in refrigerator.

Variations: Additional ingredients that may be added to the dry mixture:

½ to 1 tsp. spice of choice
1 tsp. dulse flakes, or kelp granules
¼ tsp. vitamin C powder or citric acid to prevent mold

Note: The gluten adhering to the wheat or oat bran seems to become physically engulfed in the mucilage from the seeds and may be prevented from irritating the digestive tract. However, to be safe, **those who are gluten-intolerant should avoid these brans.** Rice bran may be used instead.

* Dr. Peter D'Adamo, N.D. (author of Blood Type diet books), writes that sprouting the grain deactivates the wheat germ agglutenin which can also be irritating to the intestinal wall, especially for persons with O blood type, and I think that the presoaking accomplishes this as well.

**This can ferment if held at room temperature in hot weather, so let it soak in the refrigerator when room temperature goes over 75° F.

2 Bran Cereal made with rice bran, ground flaxseed,
black currants, presoaked almonds, sliced banana, and a dusting of nutmeg.

2 Bran Cereal (contains gluten)

Serves 1

¼ c. wheat bran
¼ c. oat or rice bran
2 Tbsp. flaxseeds, ground (**or** 1 tsp. psyllium husk **or** 1 Tbsp. chia seeds)
1 c. water

Stir together dry ingredients then stir in water and let stand in a covered glass container overnight. Serve with a dash of spice, date sugar or fresh fruit or plumped fruit and nut milk.

Variations: Replace water with nutmilk, cover and let soak in the fridge overnight. Add any of the following to the bran mixture and presoak: 1 to 2 Tbsp. raisins, currants, dried berries or chopped dried fruit; ½ to 1 tsp. dulse flakes.

Blueberry/Nectarine Breakfast

Blueberry/Nectarine Breakfast

Serves 1

Combine in a bowl:

½ c. *Precious Gump* (wheat bran/psyllium version is pictured)
1 nectarine, sliced
a handful of fresh blueberries

Place the cereal in the bowl first, then layer fruit over it. Serve with nut milk.

Mango/Coconut Breakfast with bee pollen

Mango/Coconut Breakfast

Serves 1

Combine in a bowl:
½ c. *Precious Gump*
½ mango, cubed
a handful of coconut, unsulphured, unsweetened
1 tsp. bee pollen* (optional)

Place gump in bowl and layer mango on top. Sprinkle with coconut and bee pollen. Serve with nut milk.

* Bee pollen is another super food-- rich in B-vitamins, protein, enzymes, boron needed for calcium absorption, and natural antihistamines. Use local bee pollen to combat pollen allergies. Start with ¼ tsp. or less and increase to 1 tsp. to 1 Tbsp. daily.

Hot Bran Cereals

These cereals are a pleasant change in cold weather, when time does not permit overnight soaking, or just for variety. They are served warm though they are not truly cooked. If **not** *eaten everyday, the mineral binding phytates, still intact in the bran, should pose no problem. Eating vitamin C rich foods at the same time will also deactivate the phytic acid.* **Note:** *Most red fruits and veggies contain vitamin C.*

Oat Bran Cereal *(contains gluten)*
Serves 1

1 c. boiling water
⅓ to ½ c. oat bran

Whisk the bran into the boiling water. Cover the pot and remove from heat. Let stand for 5 to 10 minutes before serving.

Variation: Stir in your favorite additions before covering.

This is a lighter and brighter variation of the previous recipe.

Oat Bran/Flaxseed Cereal *(contains gluten)*
Serves 1

1 c. water
¼ c. oat bran
2 Tbsp. flaxseeds, ground
1 tsp. to 1 Tbsp. date sugar

Bring ¾ c. water to a boil in a small covered saucepan. Combine dry ingredients in a small bowl, then stir in ¼ c. room temperature water. Whisk this mixture into boiling water. Immediately remove from heat, cover and let stand for 5 minutes. Serve with a pinch of salt and flax seed oil, or nut milk.

Rice bran is the outer layer of the rice kernel and includes part of the rice germ. It is the part of the rice kernel that is removed to make white rice. It contains natural dietary fiber, essential fatty acids, including heart healthy gamma oryzanol, B-complex vitamins (thiamine, niacin and B6) and iron.

Quick Rice Bran Cereal *(gluten free)*

Yields 1 cup

½ c. rice bran
1 c. boiling water

Whisk bran into boiling water. Immediately remove from heat, cover and let stand for 5 to 10 minutes. Serve with a dash of salt and flax seed or olive oil, or your favorite nut or seed milk.

Variations: To sweeten and flavor, stir in 2 Tbsp. raisins, currants, wolfberries or mulberries, unsulphured coconut, or grated carrots; or 1 Tbsp. date sugar; 1 tsp. dulse flakes or a little salt; spice of your choice.

A version of this is even fed to race horses to lighten them up before a race!

Hot Bran "Mash" *(contains gluten)*

Serves 1

½ c. raw wheat bran
2 Tbsp. ground flaxseeds
½ to 1 tsp. dulse flakes (optional)
1 c. boiling water
1 Tbsp. organic blackstrap molasses (optional)

In a serving bowl, mix together dry ingredients then stir in water, then molasses, if desired. Cover with a plate or lid and let stand for 15 to 20 minutes. Serve as desired.

Whole Grain Cereals

Whole grains can be presoaked and/or sprouted* to improve digestibility and to make them more palatable for raw consumption. Sprout only until the sprout reaches the length of the grain for the best flavor and tenderness. Gluten grains will still contain gluten after sprouting. Additionally, many grains are difficult to sprout or will not sprout because of age and/or hull removal. Whole grains and minimally processed grains that lend themselves to simple soaking are my personal preference, though I eat grains only occasionally.

Muesli, an uncooked grain cereal served with fresh or dried, plumped fruit, was made famous by Dr. Max Bircher-Benner, M.D. at his natural health clinic in Zürich, Switzerland, in the first half of the 20th Century.

Traditional Muesli *(contains gluten)*

Serves 1

1 c. regular oatmeal (for gluten-free, use quinoa flakes)
2 Tbsp. sunflower or pumpkin seeds
1 to 2 Tbsp. dried fruit pieces
1 c. water, or nut milk**

[handwritten margin notes: ground flax seed / craisins - dried fruit / Rice milk / fridge overnight]

Combine all ingredients and let stand overnight. In the morning, serve with fresh fruit and nut milk.

Variations: Presoak the seeds separately from the other ingredients, then drain and rinse them before combining. Replace oatmeal with rolled/ "crimped" rye, spelt or barley. Replace raisins with 1-2 Tbsp. currants, mulberries, wolfberries, date pieces or other chopped dry fruit. Stir in 1 Tbsp. chia seeds or 2 Tbsp. ground flaxseeds.

* For more information about sprouting and using raw sprouted grains, see Dr. Gabriel Cousens' *Conscious Eating.*

**The live enzymes in fresh nut milk may help to digest grains.

Buckwheat Muesli *(gluten free)*

Yields 2 cups

6 Tbsp. buckwheat groats (white, whole)
3½ Tbsp. flaxseeds, ground
4 figs, sliced, or 2 Tbsp. other dried fruit
1 tsp. dulse flakes (optional)

Combine all ingredients in a 1 pint jar. Fill with water to the top, stir, then top off with water, again. Cover and let stand overnight at room temperature. Serve with nut milk.

Quinoa Muesli *(gluten free)*

Serves 1

¼ c. quinoa flakes
1 to 2 Tbsp. chia seeds or ground flaxseeds
1 tsp. wolfberries, mulberries, raisins or currants
1 tsp. dulse flakes (optional)
6 presoaked almonds or 1 Tbsp. apricot kernels (decorticated)
1 pinch 5 Spice Powder or other spice (optional)

Combine all in a bowl. Mix with 1 cup of water and let soak for 10 to 15 minutes. Serve with your favorite "milk" and fresh fruit if desired.

Chia/Quinoa Cereal *(gluten free)*

Serves 1

½ c. *Chia Gel*
2 Tbsp. quinoa flakes

Prepare the gel ahead of time per recipe on p. 117. Stir the flakes into the gel and let stand for 5 to 10 minutes. Serve with fruit, nut milk and/or a handful of sunflower seeds.

Chapter 8

Food Storage
Tips

Food Storage Tips

Important: *Foods should be stored in clean, dry containers in dark, dry, cool locations--not under sinks, or over or beside stove tops or ovens, or in places that get warm or moist for any reason. Insects multiply quickly at temperatures above 70°F. and high humidity will encourage mold and fungal growth.*

To prevent moth and other infestations from contaminated foods, place dried fruits and grain products in the freezer for 48 hours before storing.

Bran and other grain products
Refrigerate or freeze. Rice bran and whole grains contain the germ which can go rancid if exposed to heat, light or air.

Dried Fruit
Store in glass jars in a dark, dry, cool place. Plastic or paper bags are not insect or critter-proof. Refrigerate or freeze for longest storage and best quality. Occasionally, "sugaring" will cause a granular discoloration on the surface of dried fruits like figs and prunes; this is not mold and is safe to eat.

Herbs and Spices
Fresh cut herbs should be stored in breathable bags in the refrigerator. Most dried herbs and spices may be stored at room temperature in a dark, dry place in airtight glass containers. Bulk quantities (e.g. 1 pound or more) of ground spices last longest if refrigerated or frozen, in vapor proof bags. **Note:** Ground cayenne pepper and paprika contain Vitamin A and oils, so they need to be refrigerated to prevent rancidity.

Honey, Malt and Agave Syrup
Store at room temperature. If it crystallizes, place jar in hot, not boiling water or in a warm spot until it liquefies again. (See more about these sweeteners and others in **Appendix 1**.)

Maple Syrup

This will mold if not refrigerated, frozen or canned. To can, just bring syrup to a boil, pack into clean containers and affix sterilized lids. Remove maple syrup from metal cans when you break the seal, and pour into a glass jars, to protect its flavor over time.

Nuts and Seeds

Shells protect nuts and seeds from light, heat, moisture and air. For this reason unshelled nuts and seeds store better than shelled. Shelled nuts and seeds can be refrigerated in tight containers for a few months. Nuts may be frozen for up to 2 years; seeds for a year or more. Canned nuts will keep 1 year. Almonds and filberts (hazelnuts) can be stored for a few months at room temperature.

Note: Shelled almonds and filberts (also, hazelnuts) are the most stable nuts and may be stored at room temperature for several weeks or months. Whole chia seeds and flaxseeds have a protective hull and do not require refrigeration until this hull is broken. Psyllium husk can be stored at room temperature indefinitely.

Nut and Seed Butters

Store in a dry, cool place or in the refrigerator in tightly sealed glass containers to prevent rancidity. Keep a small amount in the kitchen cabinet for daily use, if desired. If oil comes to the top, stir before refrigerating or using. Store jar inverted, with lid tightly affixed, to slow this natural separation.

Sea Vegetables (Dried)

These will store indefinitely in tightly sealed containers in a dark dry place.

Vegetable Oils

Light, heat and air turn oils rancid. Buy cold-pressed oils and store in the refrigerator. Olive oil will not flow when very cold, so keep some at room temperature in a small, preferably amber, or in a dark place.

Appendix 1

Culinary Salts
and
Sweeteners

Culinary Salts

Salt has become commonplace but it was once a valued commodity. Sodium is one of the mineral electrolytes found in healthy blood. It helps to maintain proper tissue hydration, lubricates our joints and is essential for the formation of HCl—stomach acid. In cuisine it enhances flavors and controls bacteria levels in pickling and curing. Salting food while it is raw state, will draw moisture out of it. Salting meats, beans and other protein foods while cooking will toughen them.

It is best to never cook salt, for this will change its properties making it inorganic and difficult for the body to remove, thus allowing it to build up, resulting in problems. For this reason, I encourage you to salt only after cooking, preferably at the table, and each to his/her own taste. Reheat salted foods carefully, so as not to boil them.

Natural sodium is available in fruits and vegetables, especially sea vegetables where it comes to us in a readily assimilable plant matrix with natural iodine and a wide array of macro and micro (trace) minerals. Soaking and/or rinsing dried sea veggies under running water before use will rid them of excess sodium.

Ordinary table salt is iodized to protect us from developing iodine deficiency diseases which are especially prevalent in areas that have low soil iodide levels. This *regular* salt also contains bleach (to correct the discoloration caused by the iodine), anti-caking agents (a few grains of rice in the salt shaker accomplishes the same thing) and sometimes sugar (!). Of course, the more natural iodine source is kelp or dulse—also seaweeds. Sea salt is not naturally iodized because sun drying destroys this mineral.

But whether it contains additives or not, the most harmful aspect of processing salt is heating. Therefore I only recommend sun dried, or *solar*, sea salt. For this reason the following salts are good alternatives to ordinary table salt. These salts taste the same as regular salt.

French Atlantic (Lima) Sea Salt

Sun dried, unrefined, no additives, no preservatives.

Contains per ¼ tsp. (1 g) serving: 330 mg. Sodium, 2% Daily Value for Magnesium

Available *iodized* also.

Product of France

For more information, call (888)400-LIMA (5462)
Lima nv, Industrielaan 11a
9990 Maldegem-BELGIUM
organic@limafood.com
www.limafood.com

Celtic Sea Salt®

This light grey, mineral-rich salt is hand-harvested from the clay soil of salt ponds using the 2,000 year old tradition of salt farming. It is naturally dried by the sun and wind, and retains some ocean moisture, which helps to lock in many vital trace elements, according to their website.

The Grain and Salt Society
4 Celtic Drive
Arden, N.C. 28704
800-TOP-SALT (867-7258)
www.celtic-seasalt.com

Sweeteners

Yes, we depend on our *sweet buds* to tell us when foods are ripe—at their nutrient peak—so it is natural for us to be attracted to the sweet taste. It is only when it is denatured and removed from its nutrient source, as in the case of refined concentrated sweeteners, that we get into trouble—and what trouble!!

Today we have a diabetes epidemic in the U.S. Part of the problem is that we are overdoing sugars and refined grain products. Diabetes is one of the most frightening and debilitating diseases on the planet and one of the most preventable and reversible (for Type II diabetes).

We need to find ways of satisfying our taste buds and appetites without concentrated sweeteners like sugar and high fructose corn syrup which have dulled our taste receptors. Then we will begin to enjoy the subtleties of natural flavors again. When concentrated sweeteners are desired, the following are lower impact alternatives*. They offer less total sugar and more nutrients than refined white sugar which is 99% sucrose.

Fresh or Plumped Fruits, Fruit and Veggie Purees and Juices—offer flavor, nutrients and moisture. See plumping directions in **Chapter 3**.

Agave Syrup—a low glycemic sweetener made from the agave cactus. Available from *Agave International, Crimson Dragon* or *Young Living* (see Sources in **Appendix 2)**.

Barley malt (contains gluten)—derived from toasted, sprouted barley; is 65% maltose. It has about ¼ the sweetness of refined white sugar. It is also referred to as diastatic malt and is a dough conditioner preferred by many bakers.

---

* For more about the problems caused by sugar and how to use the better sweeteners, see *Get the Sugar Out,* by Ann Louise Gittleman.

Tip: Combining *Chia Gel* 50/50, with any puree or liquid sweetener will buffer sugars while adding fiber and nutrients. Shelf life is up to 2 weeks.

Blackstrap Molasses (unsulphured)—a by-product of sugar refining. It contains as little as 35% sucrose (depending upon the processor) and is a rich source of minerals, especially calcium and iron (see chart, p. 156). The downside is pesticide residues, so use only organic products.

Brown Rice Syrup (some contains gluten)*—is a mild sweetener, made by fermenting brown rice and reducing it to a thick syrup. Nutritionist Phyllis A. Balch (author of *Prescription for Dietary Wellness*) considers it a good form of sugar for those with diabetes.

Date Sugar—This "sugar" is actually dried ground dates. As such, it has most of the nutrients intact—fiber and minerals--but doesn't melt or dissolve like sugar in baking; it will appear as little flecks of brown. Stir into hot cereal or sprinkle on top and allow to soften for a couple of minutes before eating. It is 65% fructose and sucrose.

Local Honey (unpasteurized)—75% glucose and fructose. Buy local if possible for its beneficial, desensitizing pollen. I recommend that it be unpasteurized to protect it's live enzymes. This kind of honey will crystallize. Of all the sweeteners, raw honey is perhaps the most beneficial – it has anti-bacterial and curative qualities. Use half as much as sugar for the same sweetness.

Maple Syrup or Sugar—the darker varieties are the highest in minerals. Syrup is 65% sucrose.

Sorghum Molasses—made by a similar process as blackstrap molasses but is much lower in nutrients. Buy organic.

Rapadura—is minimally processed sugar, containing 82% sucrose. It is the dried juice of sugar cane and contains all of the nutrients that have been refined out in other sugars—including chromium which helps with sugar metabolism. It is a little lighter in color than brown sugar, which is merely refined white sugar with molasses added. *Sucanat*™—sugar cane natural, is organically grown.

Rice Bran Syrup—was recommended by Dr. Bernard Jensen and is high in B-complex vitamins.

Stevia—a sweetener derived from an herb (ragweed family, in case there is sensitivity) that is 30 times sweeter than sugar and has no calories. The syrup is easiest to use. A drop or two will sweeten a cup of tea.

---

* Barley malt is sometimes used in the fermentation process.

Nutrients in *Sucanat*™
by *Wholesome Sweeteners*

1 tsp.= 4g

Calories 15
Total fat 0g
Sodium 0mg
Potassium 10mg
Calcium 6% (80 mg)
Total Carbohydrates 4g
Sugars 4g
Protein 0g

Nutrients in Organic Blackstrap Molasses

1 Tbsp. = 22g

Calories 80
Total Fat 0g
Sodium 0% (.66mg)
Potassium 730 mg
Calcium 115 mg
Magnesium 8% (32 mg)
Vitamin B₆ 10% (.2 mg)
Iron 15 % DV (2.86 mg)
Total Carbohydrate 14g
Sugars 10g

From the website of Wholesome Sweeteners, Inc.
Sugarland, Tx 77478
1-800-680-1896.
www.wholesomeSweeteners.com

% refers to the US FDA's Daily Values as listed on the label. My computations are in parentheses.

F.Y.I.: The label on Plantation™ Blackstrap Molasses (Unsulphured), manufactured by Allied Old English, Inc., states that the nutrients per tablespoon are as follows: 42 calories, 11 g. sugar, 297 mg. Potassium, 200 mg. Calcium and 3.6 mg. (20%) Iron. This product is not labeled "organic" and therefore could contain pesticide residues. Differences in growing conditions and processing might account for the nutritional differences.

Appendix 2

Sources

Sources

Kitchen Tools and Appliances

Cutco—Known for quality knives and kitchen utensils; call to have a representative visit your home.
1116 East State Street
Olean, N.Y. 14760
800-828-0448

Saladmaster, Inc.—Source for the Saladmaster "Kitchen Machine," a hand crank grater/slicer with 5 cutting cones. Sold through home parties. Home office in Arlington, Texas. (I have seen them on *ebay*, also.)
800-765-5795
http://www.saladmaster.com

WaterWise—Affordable counter-top water distillers and shower filters and accessories.
PO Box 494000
Leesburg, Fl. 34749-4000
800-874-9028
www.waterwise.com

Home Depot--Reverse Osmosis water treatment units for under-the-counter. Check the yellow pages for a store near you.

Natural Foods, Herbs, Spices and Products

Aerobic Life Industries, Inc.—source of stabilized oxygen products.
2800 E. Chambers St., Suite 700
Phoenix, AZ 85040
800-798-0707
www.aerobiclife.com

Agave International, Inc.—source of agave (low glycemic) syrup.
Los Angeles, CA 90232
310-733-4343
www.sweetcactusfarms.com

Bazaar of India Imports—Ayurvedic herbs, spices and products.
1810 University Ave.
Berkeley, CA 94703
800-261-7662

Body Ecology—live bacteria starters for cultured foods.
Atlanta, GA
1-866-KEFIR-4-U (1-866-533-4748)
www.bodyecologydiet.com

Crimson Dragon Herbs Co.—for wolfberries, decorticated apricot kernels, lotus seeds, agave syrup, alkalinizing water filters, Chinese and natural foods and herbs.
631 Ken Pratt Blvd.
Longmont, CO 80501
303-845-4877
www.herbsofwellness.com

ENER-G FOODS, INC.—gluten-free foods including baked products.
P.O. Box 84487
Seattle, WA 98124-5787
800-331-5222
www.ener-g.com

Food Directions, Inc.—maker of Tinkyada rice pastas that cook up with a texture as good as traditional wheat varieties, look for it in your natural foods store.
150 Milner Ave., Units 21-23
Scarborough, Ontario
M1S 3R3 Canada
www.tinkyada.com

Frontier Natural Products Co-op—seaweeds, chia seeds, herbs, spices, organic essential oils and more.
3021 78th St., P.O. Box 299
Norway, IA 52318
800-669-3275
www.frontiercoop.com

Gaiam, Inc.—a mail order source (Harmony) for reverse osmosis and other water filtration systems, including shower filters; full spectrum lighting, including fluorescent tubes; indoor and outdoor composting systems; eco-friendly produce bags; organic cotton and other natural fiber products; seventh generation eco-friendly clean-ing products and much more.
360 Interlocken Blvd., Ste. 200
Broomfield, CO 80021
800-869-3446
www.gaiam.com

The Grain and Salt Society—source of Celtic Sea Salt®, organically grown whole grains, nuts and seeds, including chia seeds and super nutritious *Styrian* pumpkin seeds and oil.
4 Celtic Drive
Arden, NC 28704
800-TOP-SALT (867-7258)
www.celtic-seasalt.com

Glutino Foods—gluten-free foods including baked products.
3750 Francis Hughes
Laval, Quebec H7L 5A9
800-363-DIET
www.glutino.com

The Heritage—source for Edgar Cayce books and products and much more; ask for their catalog. (Home of the *Heritage Café.*)
Dept. C, P.O. Box 444
Virginia Beach, VA 23458-0444
800-TO-CAYCE (862-2923)
www.caycecures.com

Maine Coast Sea Vegetables—the first sea vegetable processor to receive organic certification for its harvesting and handling procedures, a Socially Responsible Business Award winner in 2004; source of wildcrafted, certified organic seaweed and their new recipe book *Sea Vegetable Celebration.*
3 Georges Pond Rd.
Franklin, ME 04634
207-565-2907
http://www.seaveg.com

MENU 4 LIFE—source of raw bulk chia seeds (5 lbs. or more) and research and development of commercial uses. They provide valuable information and all of the recipes fom *The Magic of Chia,* by James F. Scheer.
25 Palatine, #120
Irvine, CA 92612
(949) 387-4992
http://menu4life.anthill.com

Quinoa Corporation—source of Ancient Harvest, organically grown quinoa and corn products.
P.O. Box 279
Gardena, CA 90248
310-217-8125
www.quinoa.net

Rising Tide Sea Vegetables—a cottage industry on the north coast of California, a source of organic seaweed including sea palm, also seaweed derived body care products.
P.O. Box 1914
Mendocino, CA 95460
707-964-5663
www.loveseaweed.com

StarWest Botanicals—retailers of certified organic herbs, spices, teas, essential oils and dehydrated soups and veggies.
11253 Trade Center Dr.
Rancho Cordova, CA 95742
888-369-4372
www.starwest-botanicals.com

Udo Erasmus—source of books and research about diet, oils and essential fatty acids. Products include Udo's Choice optimal omega-3/6 oil blend.
www.udoerasmus.com

Young Living Essential Oils—for wolfberries products, including Berry Young JuiceTM, plus agave syrup and high grade essential oils. You may refer to sponsor number 464331, Organic Annie's Wholefoods.
250 South Main St.
Payson, UT 84651
801-236-6200
www.youngliving.com

Publications

TheGreenGuide—for consumer research on organic food, safe fish and other environmentally safe consumer products, available in paper or as an e-subscription.
POB 567
New York, NY 10012
www.thegreenguide.com

Sully's Livng Without—a practical and cutting-edge magazine for people with food allergies and intolerances.
Prince Street Station
P.O. Box 2126
Northbrook, IL 60065
www.LivingWithout.com

Organizations

Celiac Disease Foundation
13251 Ventura Blvd., Ste. 1
Studio City, CA 91604-1838
818-990-2354
www.celiac.org

Celiac Sprue Association—regional support groups, "safe" foods list, newsletter, phone and online resources.
877-CSA-4-CSA
www.csaceliacs.org

Consumers Union—watchdog for the American consumer and critic of USDA's administration of the National Organic Program.
www.eco-labels.org

Demeter Association in the U.S.—certifier for biodynamic producers, source of product, grower and distributor information.
www.demeter-usa.org

Feingold Association—for dietary therapies for ADHD and learning disabilities.
www.feingold.org

Food Allergy & Anaphylaxis Network—tips for managing food allergies, alerts on allergen-containing foods, advocacy, more.
800-929-4040
www.foodallergy.org

Gluten Intolerance Group—starter patient packet, newsletter, kids camp, restaurant cards (multi-lingual), advocacy. Quick Start Dict Guidelines for new patients available online.
15110 10th Ave. SW, Ste. A
Seattle, WA 98166-1820
206-246-6652
www.gluten.net

IPM Institute of North America—label marks apples from New York and New England grown with integrated pest management (IPM).
608-232-1528
www.corevalues.org

Organic Trade Association—membership group for the organic industry, affiliated with the *Organic Center for Education and Promotion* which publishes a free e-newsletter, "The O'Mama Report."
www.ota.com
www.organic-center.org
www.theorganicreport.org
The Center
c/o OTA
P.O. 547,
Greenfield, MA 01302

Pesticide Action Network of North America (PANNA)—for an extensive pesticide database.
http://pesticideinfo.org

Slow Food, USA—a nonprofit organization started in Italy and dedicated to finding and preserving traditional methods of production and heirloom varieties; 132 chapters in the U.S. at this time.
www.slowfoodusa.org

USDA's National Organic Program Rules
www.ams.usda.gov/nop

Other Suggested Websites

Biodynamics information
www.biodynamics.com

Blood Type diet information per Peter J. D'Adamo, N.D.
www.4yourtype.com

Eden Foods Organic Manufacturer of macrobiotic, certified organic, biodynamic and Kosher foods including sea vegetables and quinoa.
www.edenfoods.com

Organic, safe food and product information
www.thegreenguide.com

The Ann Wigmore Foundation, originally in Boston, teaches *The Living Food Lifestyle*™.
P.O. Box 399 San Fidel, New Mexico 87049
(505) 552-0595
www.wigmore.org

The Fluoride Action Network
www.fluoridealert.org

Food Can Make You Ill—resources for food allergies and intolerances
www.foodcanmakeyouill.co.uk

Wheat and dairy-free recipes, Natural Health Tips, products and more (author's website)
www.organicannie.com

Sources of Organic Produce

To find Community Supported Agriculture (CSA) groups near you:
www.nal.usda.gov/afsic/csa

To find Biodynamic CSA's:
Call: 800-516-7797

To find Green Markets near you
www.ams.usda.gov/farmersmarkets/map.htm

To locate local Community Gardens:
www.communitygarden.org/links.php#Gardens

Bibliography

Abel, R. *The Eye Care Revolution, Prevent and Reverse Common Vision Problems*. rev. ed. New York, N.Y.: Kensington Publishing Corp., 2004,

Airola, P. *How To Get Well*. Phoenix, AZ.: Health Plus Publishers, 1974.

Austin, P., et al. *Food Allergies Made Simple, The Complete Manual for Diagnosis, Treatment, and Prevention of Food Allergies*. Sunfield, Michigan: Family Health Publication, 1985.

Balch, P. A., et al. *Rx Prescription for Cooking & Dietary Wellness*. Greenfield, Indiana: P.A.B. Publishing, Inc., 1987.

Baroody, T. *A. Alkalize or Die*. Waynesville, N.C.: Eclectic Press, 1991

Batmanghelidj, F. *Your Body's Many Cries For Water*. 2d ed. Vienna, VA.: Global Health Solutions, Inc., 1997

Bircher-Benner, M. *The Prevention of Incurable Disease*. Third impression. Exeter, Great Britain: A. Wheaton & Co., 1969.

Bryson, C. *The Fluoride Deception*. New York, N.Y.: Seven Stories Press, 2004.

Cichoke, A. J. *The Complete Book of Enzyme Therapy*. Garden City Park, N.Y.: Avery Publishing Group, 1999.

Cousens, G. *Conscious Eating*. Berkeley, CA.: North Atlantic Books, 2000.

D'Adamo, P.J. *Eat Right 4 Your Type*. New York, N.Y.: Penguin Putnam, Inc., 1997.

———. *Live Right 4 Your Type*. New York, N.Y.: Penguin Putnam, Inc., 2001.

Dunne, L.J. *Nutrition Almanac*, 5th ed. New York, N.Y.: McGraw-Hill, 2002.

Edgar Cayce Foundation. *An Edgar Cayce Home Medicine Guide*. Virginia Beach, VA.: ARE Press, 1982.

Erasmus, U., et al. *Fats that Heal, Fats that Kill, The Complete Guide to Fats, Oils, Cholesterol and Human Health*. Burnaby, B.C. Canada: Alive Books, 1993.

Garland, A. W. et al. *The Way We Grow, Good-Sense Solutions for Protecting Our Families from Pesticides in Food*. New York: Berkley Publishing Group, 1993.

Gates, D., et al. *The Body Ecology Diet.* Atlanta, GA.: B.E.D. Publications, 1996.

Gittleman, A.L. *Get the Sugar Out.* New York, N.Y.: Crown Trade Paperbacks, 1996.

———. *Supernutrition for Women.* New York, N.Y.: Bantam Books, 1991.

———. *Your Body Knows Best.* New York, N.Y.: Pocket Books, 1996.

Grant, D. et al. *Food Combining for Health—Get Fit with Foods that Don't Fight,* 1989.

Haas, E. M., et al. *The False Fat Diet.* New York, N. Y.: Ballantine Books, 2000.

Hobbs, C. *Foundations of Health, Liver and Digestive Herbal.* Capitola, CA.: Botanica Press, 1992.

Howell, E. *Enzyme Nutrition, The Food Enzyme Concept.* Wayne, N.J.: Avery Publishing Group, 1985.

Jensen, B. *The Healing Power of Chlorophyll from Plant Life.* Escondido, CA.: Bernard Jensen Enterprises, 1984.

Joseph, J. A., et al. *The Color Code.* New York, N. Y.: Hyperion, 2002.

Kilham, C. S. *The Bread and Circus Whole Food Bible.* Reading, MA.: Addison-Wesley Publishing Company, Inc., 1991.

Langer, S., et al. *Solved the Riddle of Illness.* Rochester, VT.: Healing Arts Press, 1989.

———. *Solved the Riddle of Weightloss.* New Canaan, CT.: Keats Publishing, Inc., 1984.

Margen, S., et al. *The Wellness Encyclopedia of Food and Nutrition.* New York, N.Y.: Rebus, Inc., 1992.

Margen, S., et al. *Wellness Foods A-Z.* New York, N.Y.: Rebus, Inc., 2002.

Miller-Cohen, A.M. *Organic Annie's Natural Health Tips & Recipes.* Baldwinsville, N.Y.: Earth Angel Publishing, 2000.

Nelson, D. *Food Combining Simplified.* Box 2302, Santa Cruz, CA, 95063, 1983.

Rapp, D. J. *Allergies and Your Family.* New York, N.Y.: Sterling Publishing Co., Inc., 1980.

Rapp, D. *Is This Your Child?* New York, N.Y.: William Morrow and Company, Inc., 1991.

Reed, B. *Food, Teens & Behavior.* Manitowoc, WI.: Natural Press, 1983.

Ross, J. *The Diet Cure.* New York, N. Y.: Penguin Putnam Inc., 1999.

Rubin, J. S. *The Maker's Diet.* Lake Mary, FL.: Siloam, 2004.

Schechter, S. R. *Fighting Radiation and Chemical Pollutants with Foods, Herbs and Vitamins: Documented Natural Remedies That Boost Your Immunity and Detoxify.* Encinitas, CA.: Vitality, Ink. 1990,

Shelton, H. *Food Combining Made Easy.* San Antonio: Dr. Shelton's Health School, 1951.

Smith, M. D. *Going Against the Grain.* New York, N.Y.: Contemporary Books, A Division of McGraw-Hill, 2002.

Steward, H.L. et al. *Sugar Busters, Cut Sugar to Trim Fat.* Sugar Busters, LLC, 1995.

Virtue, D. *The Care and Feeding of Indigo Children.* Carlsbad, CA.: Hay House, Inc., 2001.

Weed, S. S. *Healing Wise.* Woodstock, N.Y: Ash Tree Publishing, 1989.

Weiner, M. A. *Man's Useful Plants.* New York, N.Y.: Macmillan Publishing Co., Inc., 1976.

Wigmore, A. *Be Your Own Doctor, A Positive Guide to Natural Living.* Wayne, N.J.: Avery Publishing Group, 1982.

———. *The Hippocrates Diet and Health Program.* Wayne, N.J.: Avery Publishing Group, 1984.

———. *The Wheatgrass Book,* Wayne, N.J.: Avery Publishing Group, 1985.

Williams, R.J. *Nutrition Against Disease.* New York, N. Y.: Bantam Books, 1971.

Wolcott, W.L., et al. *The Metabolic Typing Diet.* New York, N.Y.: Broadway Books, a division of Random House, Inc., 2000.

Young, R.O., et al. *The pH Miracle.* New York, N.Y.: Warner Books, 2002.

Yudkin, J. *Sweet and Dangerous.* New York, N.Y.: Bantam Books, 1972.

Cookbooks

Airola, P. *The Airola Diet and Cookbook*. Phoenix, AZ.: Health Plus Publishers, 1981.

Atlas, N. *The Wholefood Catalog, A Complete Guide to Natural Foods*. Fawcett Columbine, NY., 1988.

Bircher, M., et al. *The Raw Fruits and Vegetables Book*. New Canaan, CT.: Keats Publishing, Inc. 1977.

Bradford, P., et al. *Cooking with Sea Vegetables*. Rochester, VT.: Healing Arts Press, 1985.

Dworkin, S., et al. *Blend it Splendid*. New York, N.Y.: Bantam Books, 1973.

Edwards, L. *Baking for Health*. Garden City Park, N.Y.: Avery Publishing Group Inc., 1988.

Erhart, S. et al. *Sea Vegetable Celebrations*. Summertown, TN.: Book Publishing Company, 2001.

Fallon, S., et al. *Nourishing Traditions*. San Diego, CA.: ProMotion Publishing, 1995.

Ford, M. W., et al. *The Deaf Smith County Cookbook*. New York, N.Y.: Macmillan Publishing Co, Inc. 1973.

Gittleman, A.L. *The Fat Flush Plan*. New York, N.Y.: McGraw-Hill, 2002.

Goulart, F.S. *101 Allergy-Free Desserts*. New York, N.Y.: Simon & Schuster, Inc., 1983.

Greenberg, R., et al. *Freedom from Allergy Cookbook*. Vancouver, B.C., Canada: Blue Poppy Press. 1996.

Gusman, J. *Vegetables from the Sea: everyday cooking with sea greens*. New York, N.Y.: HarperCollins Publishers, Inc., 2003.

Hagman, B. *The Gluten-Free Gourmet, Living Well without Wheat*. New York, N.Y.: Henry Holt and Company, Inc. 1990.

Jensen, B. *Vibrant Health from Your Kitchen*. Escondido, CA.: Bernard Jensen Enterprises, 1986.

Jordan, J. *Wings of Life*. Trumansburg, N.Y.: The Crossing Press, 1976.

Kinderleherer, J. *Smart Breakfasts*. New York, N.Y.: Newmarket Press, 1989.

Kulvinskas, Viktoras. *Survival into the 21st Century*. Wethersfield, CT: Omangod Press, 1975.

Larson, G. *Better Food for Better Babies and Their Families*. New Canaan, CT.: Keats Publishing, Inc., 1972.

Lewis, S.K. et al. *Allergy & Candida Cooking Made Easy*. Coralville, IA.: Canary Connect Publications, 1996.

Mercola, J., et al. *The No-Grain Diet*. New York, N.Y.: The Penguin Group, Inc., 2002.

———. *Total Health Cookbook and Program*. Schaumburg, IL.: Mercola.com, 2004.

Meyerowitz, S. *Recipes from the Sproutman*. Great Barromgton, ME.: The Sprout House, Inc., 1990.

———. *Sprout It! One Week from Seed to Salad*. Great Barrington, ME: The Sprout House, Inc., 1994.

Potts, P. *Still Going Against the Grain*. Oregon City, OR.: Central Point Publishing, 1994.

Raichlen, S. *Miami Spice*. N.Y.: Workman Publishing, 1993.

Robertson, L., et al. *Laurel's Kitchen, A Handbook for Vegetarian Cookery and Nutrition*. New York, N.Y.: Bantam Book, 1976.

Rockwell, S.J. *Allergy Recipes*. Seattle, WA.: Nutrition Survival Press, 1990.

Romano, R. *Dining in the Raw, Cooking with the "Buff"*. Prato, Italy: Prato Publications, 1996.

Rombauer, I.S., et al. *Joy of Cooking*. New York, N.Y.: Scribner, 1997.

Scheer, J.F. *The Magic of Chia, Revival of an Ancient Wonder Food*. Berkeley, CA.: Frog Ltd., 2001.

Staff of the Wellness Kitchen, et al. *The Wellness Kitchen*. New York, N.Y.: Health Letter Associates, Rebus, Inc. 2003.

Vonderplanitz, A. *the Recipe for Living Without Disease*. Santa Monica, CA.: Carnelian Bay Castle Press, 2002.

Wigmore, A., et al. *Ann Wigmore's Recipes for a Longer Life*. Wayne, N.J.: Avery Publishing Group, 1980.

Index

"Organic Annie"

About the Author

Ann Miller-Cohen, B. A., C. Ir., has been on a *special diet* since she was diagnosed with an allergy to chocolate at age 2. The recipes in this book were developed after her own children were born, and it was discovered that she and her sons had allergies to wheat and dairy products. Other recipes were developed for *Organic Annie's Wholefoods*, her special diet foods business, for Dr. Doris Rapp, for the Heritage Store in Virginia Beach, Virginia, and to meet the special needs of clients and friends. While Ann likes to prepare foods simply, she loves to experiment with new wholesome foods.

Ann is also a Certified Iridologist and relies heavily upon her knowledge of special diet foods and nutrition to counsel her clients. She is the author of *Organic Annie's Natural Health Tips and Recipes*, a self-health guide, Earth Angel Publishing, 2000. Her website is www.organicannie.com.

She lives in the town of Manlius, just outside of Syracuse, N.Y.